Specials!

Textiles 2

Julie Messenger and Di Brown

Acknowledgements

P. 36 Elise Co, Aeolab (www.aeolab.com) (bottom left)

© 2009 Folens Limited, on behalf of the authors.

United Kingdom: Folens Publishers, Waterslade House, Thame Road, Haddenham, Buckinghamshire, HP17 8NT.
Email: folens@folens.com   Website: www.folens.com

Ireland: Folens Publishers, Greenhills Road, Tallaght, Dublin 24.
Email: info@folens.ie   Website: www.folens.ie

Folens publications are protected by international copyright laws. All rights are reserved. The copyright of all materials in this publication, except where otherwise stated, remains the property of the publisher and the authors. No part of this publication may be reproduced, stored in a retrieval system, or transmitted, in any form or by any means, for whatever purpose, without the written permission of Folens Limited, except where authorized.

Folens allows photocopying of pages marked 'copiable page' for educational use, providing that this use is within the confines of the purchasing institution. Copiable pages should not be declared in any return in respect of any photocopying licence.

Julie Messenger and Di Brown hereby assert their moral rights to be identified as the authors of this work in accordance with the Copyright, Designs and Patents Act 1988.

Commissioning editor: Paul Naish	Editor: Kate Greig
Text design and layout: Planman	Illustrator: Andy Elkerton/www.hardwickstudios.com
Cover design: Holbrook Design	Front cover image: © iStockphoto.com/DNY59

The websites recommended in this publication were correct at the time of going to press; however, websites may have been removed or web addresses changed since that time. Folens has made every attempt to suggest websites that are reliable and appropriate for students' use. It is not unknown for unscrupulous individuals to put unsuitable material on websites that may be accessed by students. Teachers should check all websites before allowing students to access them. Folens is not responsible for the content of external websites.

For general spellings Folens adheres to the *Oxford Dictionary of English*, Second Edition (Revised), 2005.

First published 2009 by Folens Limited.

Every effort has been made to contact copyright holders of material used in this publication. If any copyright holder has been overlooked, we will be pleased to make any necessary arrangements.

British Library Cataloguing in Publication Data. A catalogue record for this publication is available from the British Library.

ISBN: 978-1-85008-464-8   Folens code FD4648

Contents

Introduction	4
Targeted research	5
Research: what and how?	6
Mood boards	7
Design development	8
Market research	9
Extending the range	10
Historical influences on design	11
Decades of design	12
Crystal ball designing	13
Fashion timeline	14
The ethics of fashion	15
Designing an accessory	16
Properties, care and use of fabrics	17
Laundry symbols	18
Properties of fabrics	19
Care of fabrics (1) – laundry tests	20
Care of fabrics (2) – choosing care symbols	21
Which fabric is best for...?	22
Recycling	23
Why recycle?	24
Recycle	25
Repair	26
Reuse (1)	27
Reuse (2)	28
Adding colour to fabric	29
Where in the world?	30
Shisha work	31
Shibori dyeing	32
Jacquard or Fair Isle patterns for knitted fabrics	33
Creating a checked fabric	34

Smart and technical fabrics	35
Textile products and smart fabrics	36
Technical fabrics and microfibres	37
The use of smart and technical fabrics	38
Smart and technical fabrics... what am I?	39
Analysing a product	40
Industrial practice	41
Clothing manufacture	42
One-off, batch and mass production	43
Costing products	44
Product analysis	45
Making identical products	46
Aesthetics	47
Braiding	48
Make a braid	49
Making a fabric brooch	50
Couching	51
Accessories	52
What is an accessory?	53
Hats and their functions	54
Accessories for sport	55
Designing a cushion cover	56
Eco-friendly bags	57
Labels and logos	58
Why blend fabrics?	59
Labels explained	60
Branding: logos	61
Design a logo	62
Air miles	63
Assessment sheet	64

Introduction

Specials! Design and Technology activities are planned for students with a reading comprehension age of seven to nine years and working at levels 1 to 3. This second textiles book in the series is divided into activities that underpin the further concepts in textiles technology, including historical influences on design, industrial practices, further decorative techniques and smart and technical fabrics. It also guides students through essential activities to help them consider targeted research techniques, aesthetics and recycling issues when designing and making.

This book contains ten separate units covering the topics needed to complete the theme of the book. Each unit has one or more photocopiable Resource sheets and several Activity sheets. This allows the teacher to work in different ways. The tasks are differentiated throughout the book and offer all students the opportunity to expand their skills.

The teacher can work in different ways: each unit could be taught as one or two lessons with students working individually, in pairs or in groups. Alternatively, a single Resource sheet and related Activity sheet(s) could be used as required. Some student pages are more challenging than others so they will need to be selected accordingly.

The Teacher's notes give guidance and are laid out as follows:

Objectives
These are the main skills or knowledge to be learnt.

Prior knowledge
This refers to the minimum skills or knowledge required by students to complete the tasks. Some Activity sheets are more challenging than others and will need to be selected accordingly.

Links
All units link to the Design and Technology National Curriculum at Key Stage 3, Scottish attainment targets and the Northern Ireland and Welsh Programmes of Study.

Background
This gives additional information for the teacher about particular aspects of the topic.

Starter activity
Since the units can be taught as a lesson, a warm-up activity focusing on an aspect of the unit is suggested.

Resource sheets and Activity sheets
The Resource sheets are used as stimulus for discussion and contain no tasks or activities. Where useful, keywords are given in the Teacher's notes and related tasks are provided on the Activity sheets. Links with other Activity sheets are sometimes indicated.

Plenary
The teacher can use the suggestions here to do additional work, recap on the main points covered, or reinforce a particular point.

Assessment sheet
At the end of the book there is an Assessment sheet focusing on student progress and learning. It can be used in different ways. A student could complete it as a self-assessment, while the teacher or support assistant also complete one on the student's progress. The two can then be compared and contrasted during a discussion. Alternatively, students could work in pairs to carry out a peer-assessment and then compare outcomes.

Look out for other titles in the Design and Technology series, including:
- Designing and making
- Food
- Food 2
- Graphic products
- Product design
- Resistant materials
- Sustainable design
- Systems and control
- Textiles

Teacher's notes

Targeted research

Objectives

- To understand why research is necessary to the design process
- To learn some simple ways to undertake research
- To learn some simple ways to record research findings
- To be able to develop and extend design ideas

Prior knowledge

Students need to know that product designs come from a specific design brief and that products are designed for specific consumer markets. Students need to appreciate that designers do not design for themselves but for others.

NC links

Key concepts: 1.1 Designing and making;
1.3 Creativity
Key processes: a, h
Range and content: a, b
Curriculum opportunities: b, c

Northern Ireland PoS

Skills: Ask questions and suggest ideas for making things; Gather, evaluate and use information relevant to a design brief

Scottish attainment targets

Needs and how they are met: Level B, Level C

Welsh PoS

Skills: Designing: 2, 3

Background

This unit provides some basic tools to aid students to complete research at various stages of the design process and to develop and extend their initial ideas. This unit could form part of a full design and make project, or as a stand alone unit. Teachers should provide a range of papers, fabrics, books and magazines to stimulate ideas and to use for mood boards – Internet access is also useful. There are lots of examples of mood boards on the Internet, such as the BBC's Homes site www.bbc.co.uk/homes/design/colour_moodboard.shtml.

Starter activity

Students should be given a simple design brief, for example, design a cushion for a child's bedroom. You may also like to give a selection of themes such as sport, transport, space, pets, flowers, and so on. There could be a general discussion about stereotypical likes and dislikes before students use the sheets.

Resource sheets and Activity sheets

The Resource sheet, 'Research: what and how?', could also be used as a starter activity. Completed as a group, students could fill a further 'ring' of boxes with ideas about how they can find answers to the questions raised, or any further questions they can think of.

The following Activity sheets could be completed individually or in small groups depending on the class size.

The Activity sheet, 'Mood boards', explains how a mood board is created and why. It asks students to choose a theme and collect materials to create their own mood board.

The Activity sheet, 'Design development', gives students a basic cushion design and the opportunity to develop the design to create other cushion covers.

The Activity sheet, 'Market research', could be completed using a purchased product or a prototype made by the class; with some adaptation to the questions the sheet could also be used with a paper design.

The Activity sheet, 'Extending the range', asks students to develop a cushion design to create other products within the same design range.

Plenary

Students could compare the results of their research and discuss their findings: did all the groups have similar results? How will the information they have collected affect their designs? What will they change?

Resource sheet – Targeted research

Research: what and how?

There are lots of things you need to think about when designing a new product. You need to do research to make sure that your product will work. The following questions can help you to start your research.

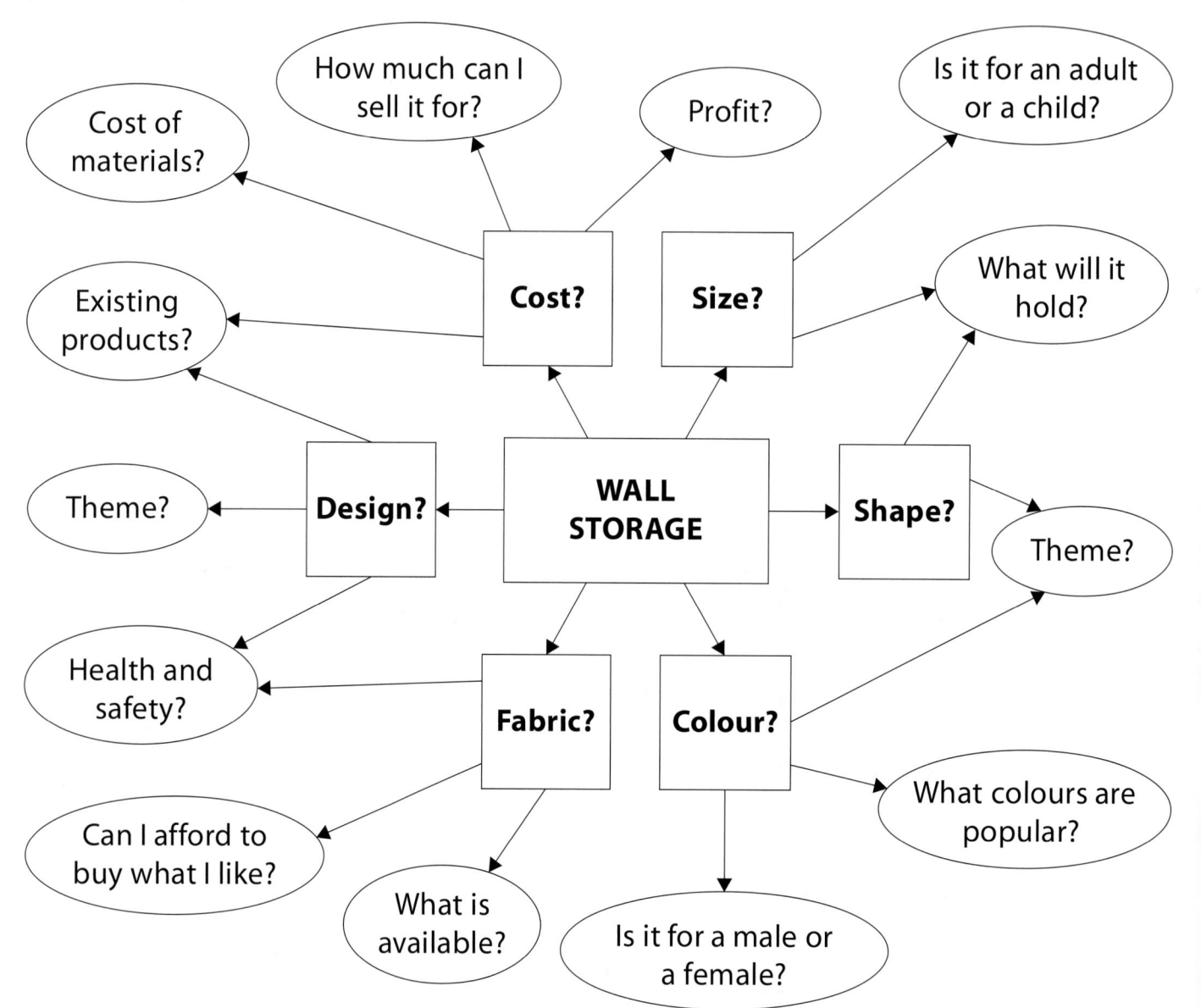

- Cost of materials?
- How much can I sell it for?
- Profit?
- Is it for an adult or a child?
- Existing products?
- What will it hold?
- Theme?
- Health and safety?
- Can I afford to buy what I like?
- What is available?
- Is it for a male or a female?
- What colours are popular?
- Theme?

Central concept: **WALL STORAGE**, connected to: Cost?, Size?, Shape?, Colour?, Fabric?, Design?

Think about how you could find answers to these questions. You could…

- Use the Internet
- Look at existing products
- Ask people who use the product (customer research)
- Look in catalogues and magazines
- Look in shops

What other ways can you think of to research your answers?

Activity sheet – Targeted research

Mood boards

A mood board is a collection of pictures and items presented as a poster or a file on a computer. Designers use a mood board to show their ideas to other people. Mood boards are based around a theme. They help you to develop your ideas.

A mood board can have:

- Coloured paper or card
- Wallpaper, postcards, wrapping paper
- Samples of fabric, ribbon or wool
- Clip-art
- Images from the Internet
- Words linked to your theme
- Pictures cut from magazines or catalogues of products, people or lifestyles

☞ Choose a theme and create your own mood board. Use materials from the list above.

Activity sheet – Targeted research

Design development

Once you have your first design idea you should spend some time developing it. This means playing, exploring and trying out new ideas, rather than using the first idea that you have. Your ideas will then be more creative and interesting.

☞ 1 You are to design a cushion cover. Your first idea has two stars on the front.

☞ 2 Sketch four more ideas in the boxes below to develop the cushion design further.

Change the colours	Change the design
Change the shape	Change the size

☞ 3 What else could you change? Record your ideas.

Activity sheet – Targeted research

Market research

When you have a design you need to know if people would buy it. To find out you could show people your drawings, or a prototype if you have made one.

☞ 1 Carry out some market research. Use the questionnaire to record people's answers.

	Yes	No
Do you like the colour?		
Do you like the size?		
Do you like the fabric?		
Would you buy it for yourself?		
Would you buy it for someone else?		

	Male	Female
Who would you buy it for?		

	Under 4 years	4–10 years	11–15 years	16–20 years	21–30 years	Over 30 years
What age group do you think would like it?						

	Under £5	£5–£10	£11–£15	£16–£20	£21–£25	Over £25
How much would you expect it to cost?						

☞ 2 Record your results as a graph to show what you have found out.

Activity sheet – Targeted research

Extending the range

Designers often make a set of products using the same design. For example, matching cushions, curtains and bedcovers.

☞ Use this cushion design as a starting point for designing a laundry bag. Draw your new design. Choose two other products and add your designs below.

Duvet cover	Laundry bag

10 Textiles 2 © Folens (copiable page)

Teacher's notes

Historical influences on design

Objectives
- To be able to adapt fashion styles from the past to create garments for the future
- To be able to identify and name fashion features from the 1940s, 1950s, 1960s and 1970s
- To know that specific social and musical events influence fashion designs

Prior knowledge
Students should be able to name parts of a garment such as collars, cuffs, pockets, fastenings, and so on. They should have an understanding of the term 'design development'. Students also need to be capable of roughly sketching garments and be confident about adapting and adjusting parts or elements of a design to create another design.

NC links
Key concepts: 1.2 Cultural understanding
Key processes: a, h
Range and content: a, d, e
Curriculum opportunities: a, b, c, e

Northern Ireland PoS
Communicating orally, graphically and in writing as a means to exploring and developing ideas
Designing: e

Scottish attainment targets
Needs and how they are met: Level C
Carrying out tasks: Level C

Welsh PoS
Skills: Designing: 1, 3
Skills: Making: 1, 3

Background

This unit looks at how design features from the past can provide inspiration for designs for the future and ensures students understand that social and musical events influence fashion.

Starter activity

Using the Resource sheet, 'Decades of design', students should see how many fashion features they can identify. Could they find one 'fashion feature' for each letter of the alphabet? For example, A = Appliqué motif; B = Belt; C = Cuff, and so on. Ask students to name or describe the key fashion features of each decade. Ask students if they can see a link between a social event and its influence on the clothing of the same decade, for example, sparkly and shiny fabrics used in the 1970s were influenced by interest in the moon landings (the first in 1969).

Discuss with students the colours used during different decades. Students could produce 'colour charts' (bands of colours arranged on small strips of paper) to represent the different decades.

Resource sheets and Activity sheets

The Activity sheet, 'Crystal ball designing', encourages students to develop design ideas using fashion features from the past to inspire them. Access to lots of coloured pictures of different fashions, various social and musical events that took place between the beginning of the 1940s and the end of the 1970s would help to make the designing task easier for students. The sheet could be photocopied and enlarged to A3 so the models are bigger.

The Activity sheet, 'Fashion timeline', requires students to cut out the cards. They should decide which fashion shapes and styles, and social and musical events fit into which decade. Students could then check each others' work. They need to be able to say why they think the answers are correct or incorrect.

The Activity sheet, 'The ethics of fashion', introduces students to a complex concept. It explores social pressures on fashion design and asks them to consider whether it is right or wrong to use certain materials when making clothes.

The Activity sheet, 'Designing an accessory', requires students to adapt an accessory to create a product from different decades.

Plenary

Students should share their designs with each other from Activity sheets, 'Crystal ball designing' and 'Designing an accessory'. They could look at features that appear in everyone's designs from a specific decade.

Students could talk about the fashion decade they would like to have lived in and why.

Resource sheet – Historical influences on design

Decades of design

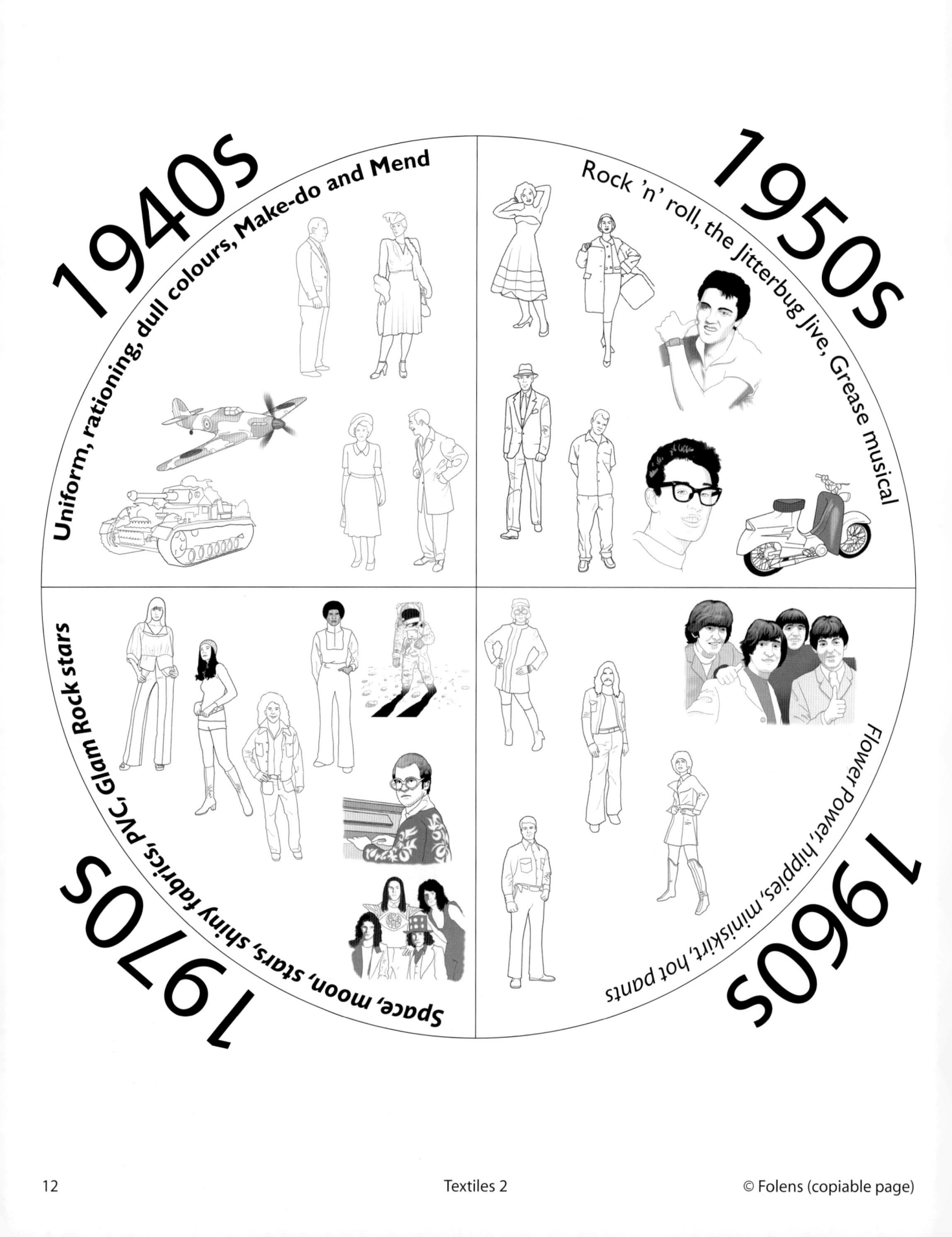

1940s — Uniform, rationing, dull colours, Make-do and Mend

1950s — Rock 'n' roll, the Jitterbug Jive, Grease musical

1970s — Space, moon, stars, shiny fabrics, PVC, Glam Rock stars

1960s — Flower power, hippies, miniskirt, hot pants

Activity sheet – Historical influences on design

Crystal ball designing

You will need to come up with ideas for male and female fashion garments for the future. When designing outfits you need to think about the age of the people you are designing for, when they will wear the outfits and what colours are suitable.

☞ Draw your designs onto the models below. You should include a front and back view for both designs. Once you are happy with your design, add colour to them.

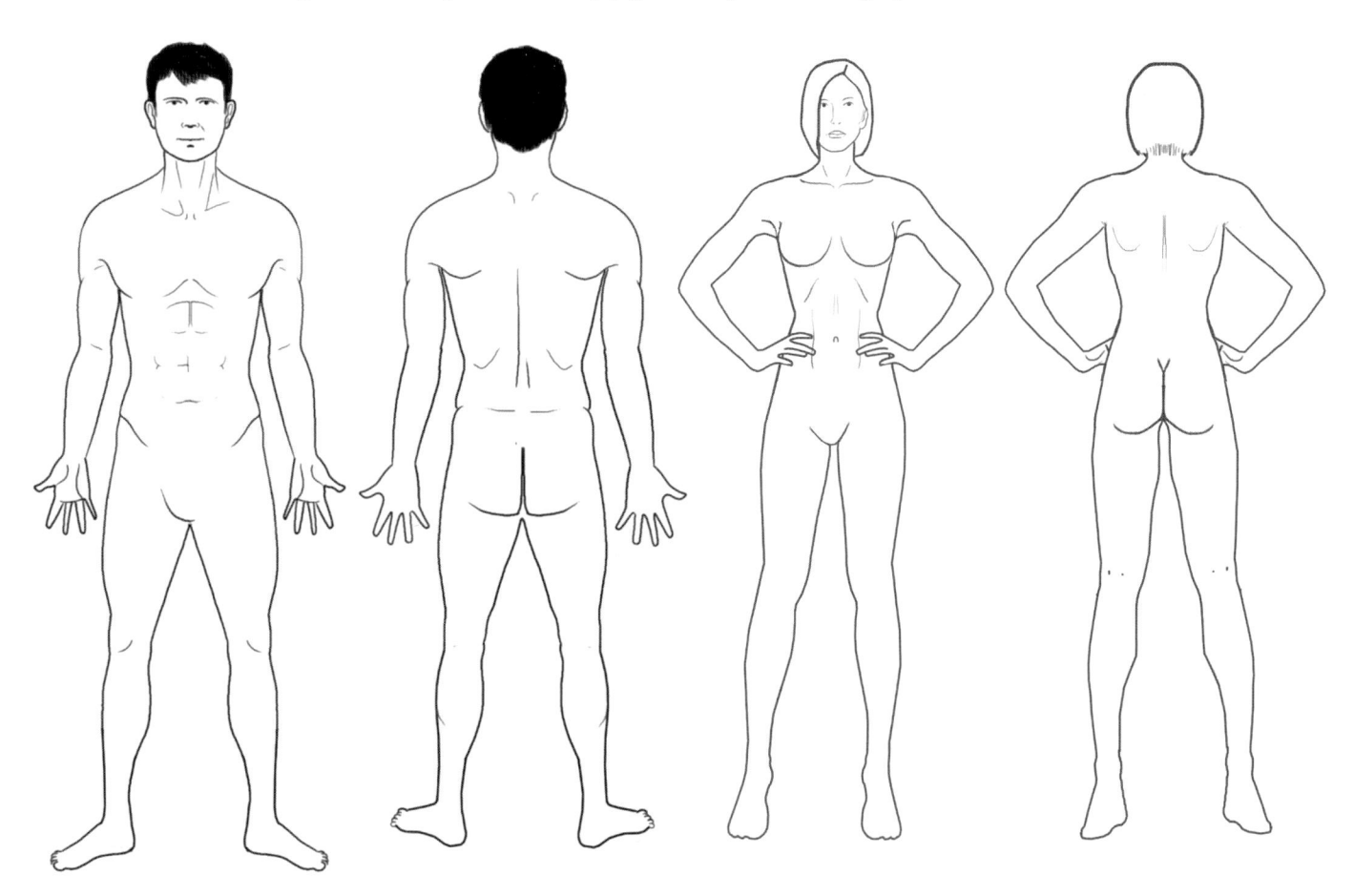

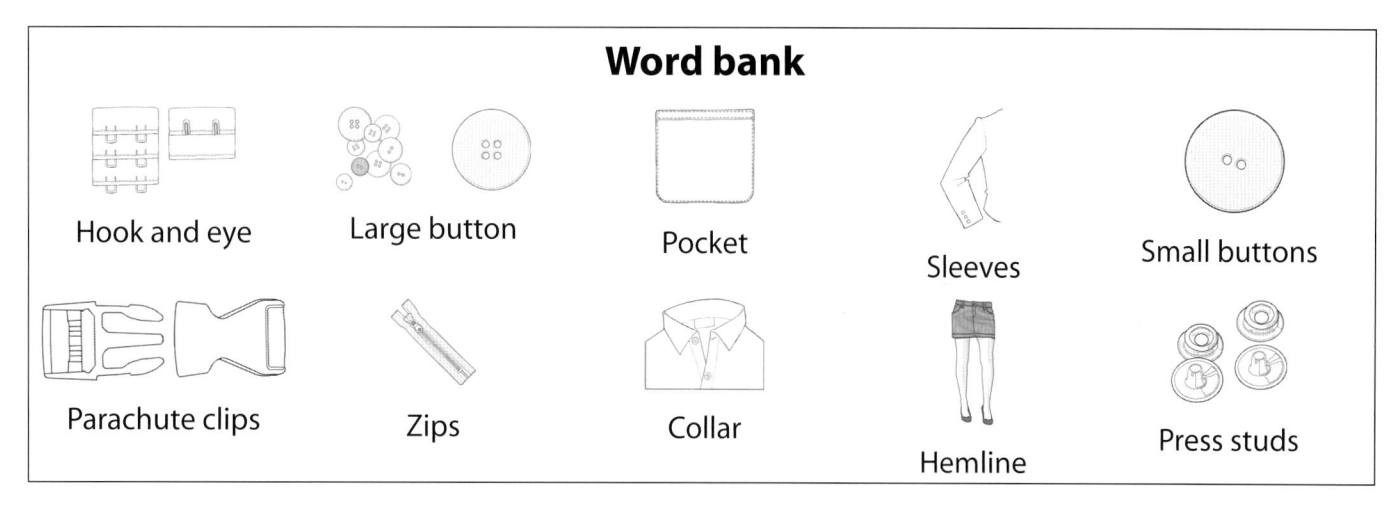

Word bank

- Hook and eye
- Large button
- Pocket
- Sleeves
- Small buttons
- Parachute clips
- Zips
- Collar
- Hemline
- Press studs

© Folens (copiable page) — Textiles 2

Activity sheet – Historical influences on design

Fashion timeline

☞ 1 Cut out the decade and picture cards.

1940s	1950s	1960s	1970s
Man landing on the moon	**Elton John**	**Buddy Holly**	**A World War II tank**
Elvis Presley	**Slade**	**The Beatles**	**A Spitfire**

☞ 2 Glue the decade cards to the top of a piece of paper. Match the pictures to the correct decade. When you are happy with your decisions, glue the images under the correct decade.

Activity sheet – Historical influences on design

The ethics of fashion

In the past some materials were used in fashion that we do not like to use now. For example, some people now think it is cruel to kill animals to make fur coats.

☞ Consider whether you think it is right or wrong to use the following materials when making clothes. Place a tick or a cross in the 'Right or wrong?' column and explain why you believe this.

Materials	Right or wrong? ✓ ✗
Coats made from animal fur.	✓ (Joe thinks that fur is natural and that animals are slaughtered for meat anyway.) ✗ (Julie thinks that people should wear synthetic fur because killing animals is cruel.)
Corsets made from whale bone.	
Buttons made from animal bone.	
Jeans made from organic cotton.	
Outdoor jackets made from fleece manufactured from recycled plastic drinks bottles.	

© Folens (copiable page)   Textiles 2

Activity sheet – Historical influences on design

Designing an accessory

An accessory is a decorative product to add to an item of clothing. Gloves, hats, bags, belts, scarves and ties are all examples of accessories. They add colour and style but can also have a practical function.

☞ Make changes to the bag design on the left so it looks like a bag from the 1940s, 1960s and 1970s. Label the changes made to each design using words from the word bank.

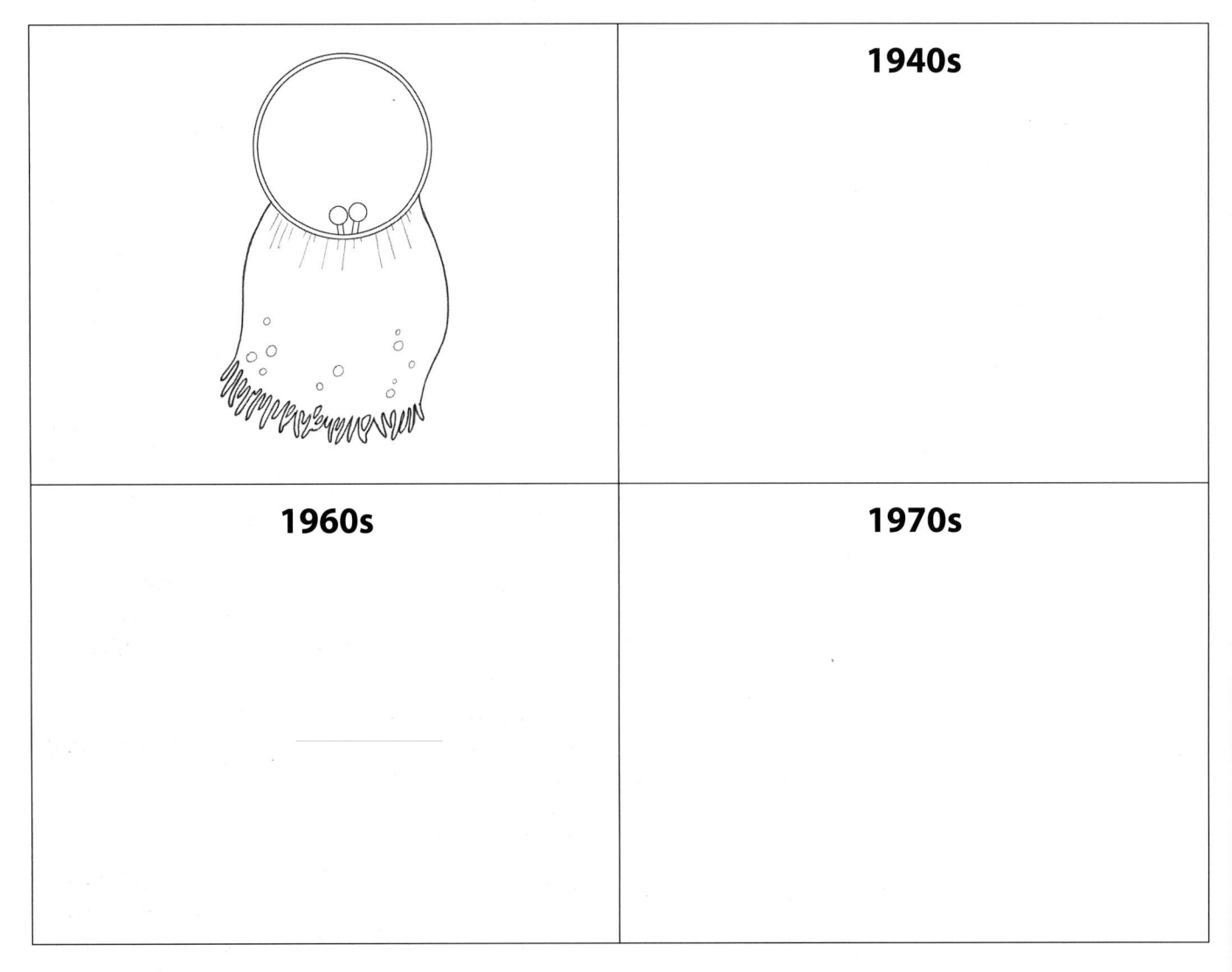

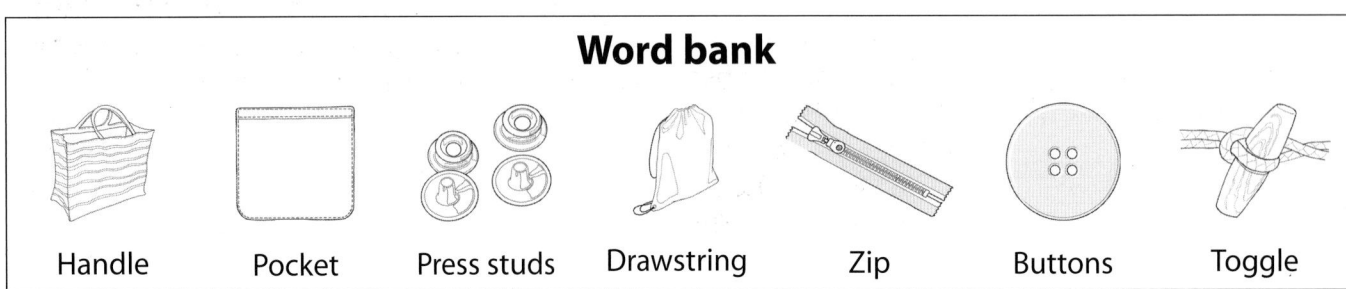

	1940s
	1960s	**1970s**

Word bank

Handle   Pocket   Press studs   Drawstring   Zip   Buttons   Toggle

16 Textiles 2 © Folens (copiable page)

Teacher's notes

Properties, care and use of fabrics

Objectives

- To understand the term 'property'
- To undertake simple tests to identify properties
- To understand that different fabrics require different care
- To undertake simple tests to determine how a fabric should be cared for
- To be able to use this information to decide on a fabric's suitability for certain products

Prior knowledge

Students need to know what a fabric is and to have experience of sorting and matching activities. They should have the opportunity to look at and handle chosen fabrics.

NC links

Key concepts: 1.1 Designing and making
Key processes: c, f
Range and content: a, e, l
Curriculum opportunities: a, b

Northern Ireland PoS

Manufacturing materials, components, techniques and processes

Scottish attainment targets

Resources and how they are managed: Level C, Level D

Welsh PoS

Skills: Designing: 2
Skills: Making: 10, 11

Background

This unit focuses on students being able to use simple observations and testing to analyse fabrics, and the best ways in which to use and care for them. Teachers should select two fabrics with obviously different properties, care needs or uses – denim and voile have been used on the Activity sheets, but these could be substituted with any other suitable fabrics.

Starter activity

Each student should be given one large piece of each fabric (at least 20–30cms square) to look at and handle. There should be a group discussion about properties of fabrics that students have looked at previously. Students could also look at a number of products made with each type of fabric, taking note of the similarities and differences between the types of product that each fabric is used for.

Resource sheets and Activity sheets

Students should work with several small samples of each fabric and carry out the individual tests to complete each Activity sheet.

The Resource sheet, 'Laundry symbols', introduces students to washing instruction labels and their meanings.

The Activity sheet, 'Properties of fabrics', requires each student to have shallow and deep containers for water, an elastic band and two different types of fabric. Students should stretch the fabrics across the water container and see if they soak up water, are waterproof or change shape. Students could record their results in the table.

The Activity sheet, 'Care of fabrics (1) – laundry tests', asks students to record what happens to the different fabrics when different tests are carried out on them. This could be completed as a group testing session, or as homework.

The Activity sheet, 'Care of fabrics (2) – choosing care symbols', asks students to decide which care symbols would need to appear on the washing labels of each fabric.

The Activity sheet, 'Which fabric is best for…?', requires students to consider which fabric is best used to make different products.

Plenary

Students should compare their findings and discuss why a fabric's properties or care requirements might make it more or less suitable for a particular use. A follow-up activity could be to make a small bag from each fabric – choosing the most appropriate style for each using the information they have learnt.

Resource sheet – Properties, care and use of fabrics

Laundry symbols

These laundry symbols are found on care labels. They represent simple washing instructions so that you can clean and dry the fabric correctly. If you do not follow the instructions the fabric may shrink, lose shape or lose colour.

This fabric can be washed in a washing machine. The number tells you what temperature the water should be.

This fabric must be washed by hand.

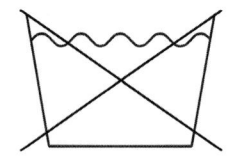

This fabric cannot be washed at all.

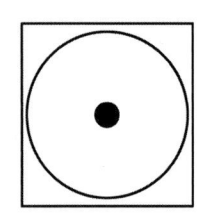

This fabric can be tumble-dried. One dot means a warm setting, two dots mean a hot setting.

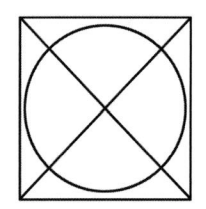

This fabric cannot be tumble dried.

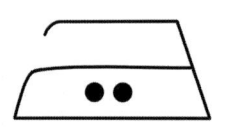

This symbol tells you how hot to set the iron. One dot is cool, two dots is warm, three dots is hot. If the iron is crossed out, do not iron the fabric.

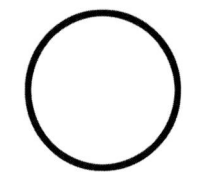

This fabric must be dry-cleaned.

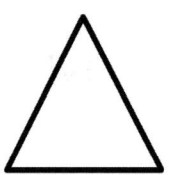

This fabric can be cleaned with bleach. If it is crossed out, do not use bleach.

Activity sheet – Properties, care and use of fabrics

Properties of fabrics

When choosing which fabric to use for a product, you may want one that is waterproof or stretchy. The two fabrics you will be testing are very different. How would you describe them – warm, soft, rough, stiff? Test the fabric samples and see what properties they have.

☞ 1 Stick a small example piece of each fabric in the correct box below.

Denim	**Voile**

☞ 2 Carry out the following tests on your two pieces of fabric to find out their properties. Record your findings below.

What to test	Question	Denim	Voile
Is it absorbent? Put a teaspoon of water in a dish. Put your fabric on the top.	Does the fabric soak up water?	Yes/No	Yes/No
Is it waterproof? Use an elastic band to hold your fabric over a jar. Pour a teaspoon of water onto the fabric.	Does the fabric stop the water coming through?	Yes/No	Yes/No
Does it stretch? Hold two corners of your fabric and pull hard.	Does your fabric change shape and size when pulled?	Yes/No	Yes/No

Activity sheet – Properties, care and use of fabrics

Care of fabrics (1) – laundry tests

Using a piece of denim and a piece of voile, you are going to do some tests to find out how to look after them.

☞ Take some sample pieces of the two different fabrics and try the tests below to see how the materials react. Record your findings in the table.

Laundry test	Denim	Voile
Wash in a washing machine at 30 degrees		
Wash by hand in warm water		
Dry in a tumble dryer		
Iron using a hot iron		
Iron using a cool iron		

Activity sheet – Properties, care and use of fabrics

Care of fabrics (2) – choosing care symbols

☞ Think about your test results from the Activity sheet, 'Care of fabrics (1) – laundry tests'. Using the Resource sheet, 'Laundry symbols', to help you, create care labels for each fabric below. What symbols do you need to use?

Denim

Voile

Activity sheet – Properties, care and use of fabrics

Which fabric is best for... ?

☞ Using what you have learnt about fabrics, choose which would be the best fabric to use to make each of the following products. Stick a small piece of the fabric next to the product and write the name of the fabric underneath it.

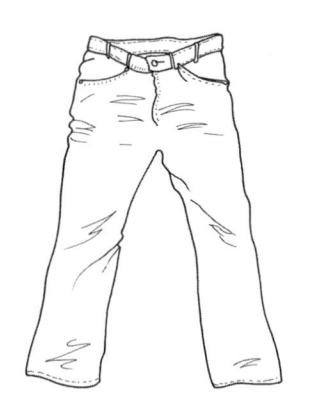

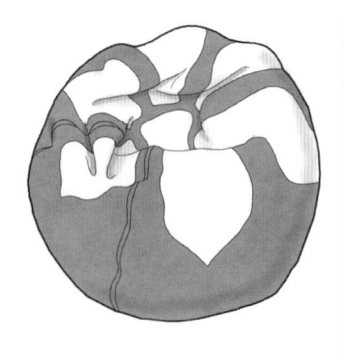

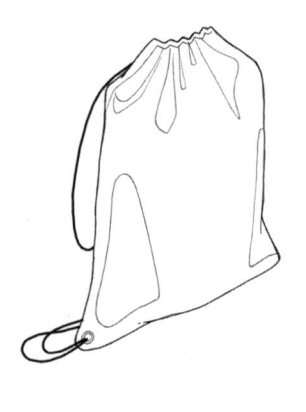

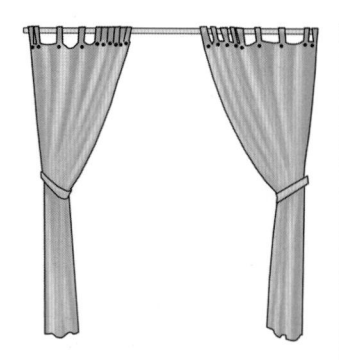

22 Textiles 2 © Folens (copiable page)

Teacher's notes

Recycling

Objectives

- To be able to identify if a product can be repaired, reused or recycled
- To be able to identify an appropriate method of repair, reuse, remodelling or recycling
- To be able to carry out some of these methods

Prior knowledge

Students should understand the reasons why recycling is necessary. Students should be able to carry out basic hand and machine sewing, and use basic equipment safely.

NC links

Key concepts: 1.1 Designing and making
Key processes: h
Range and content: a, d, e
Curriculum opportunities: a, b

Northern Ireland PoS

Designing as an imaginative and creative activity which brings together knowledge and understanding of communication techniques, materials and components, manufacturing processes, and the use of energy and control

Scottish attainment targets

Resources and how they are managed: Level B, Level C, Level D

Welsh PoS

Skills: Designing: 4, 8
Skills: Making: 15

Background

This unit focuses on students being able to use their judgement to decide how best to prevent fabric and used fabric products from being thrown away. It will give a range of ways to rethink the use of fabric and discourage 'throwaway' attitudes to worn items.

Starter activity

Each student, or small group of students, should have access to a range of old garments (some with holes or stains) and a range of fabrics that can be used. Students should sort through the samples and discuss whether they should be repaired, altered, made into a new product or completely recycled. They may also like to use books and the Internet to look at the work of designers who use recycled textiles. The BBC website www.bbc.co.uk/blast/browse (search for 'recycling') may provide inspiration, as may www.wasteonline.org.uk/resources/InformationSheets/Textiles.htm.

Resource sheets and Activity sheets

The Resource sheet, 'Why recycle?', can be used to prompt discussion about throwaway fashion versus recycling clothes.

The Resource sheet, 'Recycle', highlights ways in which fabrics can be recycled and could be used for ideas and discussion, or some of the suggestions could be carried out.

Students should complete the Activity sheet, 'Repair', and discuss any problems or anything they have noticed, for example, is one type of fabric more suitable than another for appliqué repairs?

Students could use the Resource sheet, 'Reuse (1)', as a stimulus to create a range of their own designs, which could be made if appropriate.

The Activity sheet, 'Reuse (2)', could be completed individually or in groups of four with the sheet passed on to the next person in the group for each stage of the process, resulting in a group design. The designs can then be discussed and one or more bags made. There could then be discussion about how other garments could be rethought to make completely different products.

Plenary

Students should compare their work and evaluate what they have done. They should be encouraged to consider whether their views about recycling clothes, particularly those not currently in fashion, have changed.

A follow-up activity could be to hold a recycle fashion show or to make recycled rugs, shopping bags or patchwork quilts as an enterprise activity.

Resource sheet – Recycling

Why recycle?

Did you know…

> Approximately one million tonnes of textiles are thrown away every year.

> Textile recycling started in the Yorkshire Dales about 200 years ago. Unwanted textiles were collected by the rag-and-bone man.

> Three per cent of the weight of an average household bin consists of textiles.

> Fifty per cent of textiles that are thrown away could be recycled.

Clothes that are thrown away could be resold or used elsewhere. For example, clothes could be reused by people in areas where there are emergencies such as floods or earthquakes.

Other textile materials can be used by the flocking industry to make insulation and roofing felt. They can also be used by the wiping industry to make wiping cloths used in industry. Reclaimed silk and cotton can be used to make paper.

> If every person in the UK bought one reclaimed woollen garment each year, it would save an average of 371 million gallons of water and 480 tonnes of chemical dyes.

Resource sheet – Recycling

Recycle

Fabrics can be taken apart or recycled and turned into new products. The table below shows you some of the ways fabric can be recycled.

Patchwork Cut shapes from pieces of fabric and sew them together to make quilts and cushions.	**Proddy rugs** Cut strips of fabric and poke them through holes in a piece of hessian to make a rug.
Plaiting Long strips of fabric can be plaited together then coiled and stitched to make mats.	**Coiling** Wrap long strips of fabric around a length of rope. Coil and stitch to make mats.
Weaving Strips of fabric can be woven by hand or on a loom to make mats and rugs.	**Crocheting** Long thin strips of fabric can be crocheted, just like wool.
Knitting Long thin strips of fabric can be knitted to make cushions, rugs and clothes.	

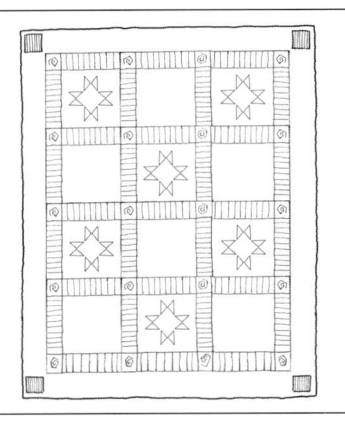

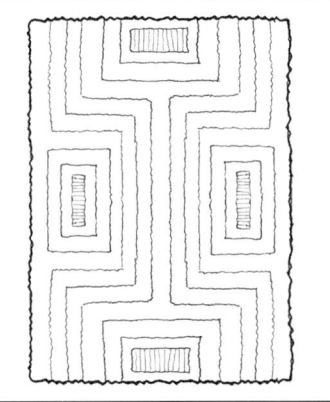

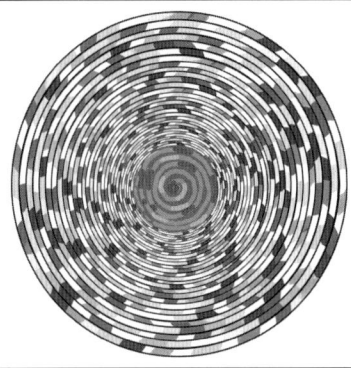

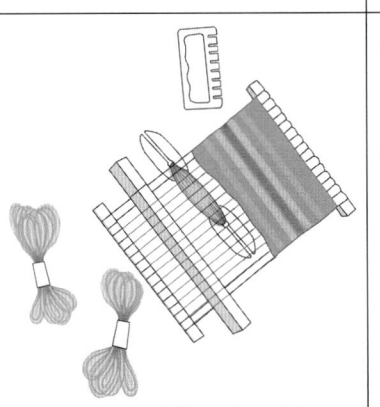

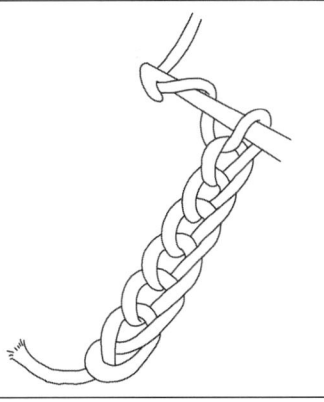

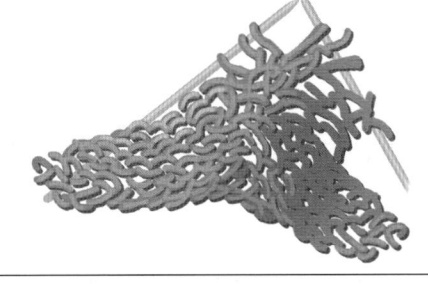

Did you know you can also recycle carrier bags? Just cut them into long thin strips and knit them into shopping bags.

Activity sheet – Recycling

Repair

Holes or tears in clothes can be repaired using a method called appliqué. You can create your own motif from a patterned fabric, or you can buy ready-made motifs.

☞ Select a piece of material with a hole in it. Choose some different fabric to cover the hole and follow the instructions below.

1 Measure the hole.	
2 Choose a shape.	
3 Cut the shape out of card. Make sure it is big enough to cover the hole.	
4 Cut out the shape and the iron-on fusible interfacing.	
5 Put your shape over the hole and iron it into place.	
6 Sew the shape down using a running stitch or a zigzag stitch.	

Resource sheet – Recycling
Reuse (1)

Clothes that you don't wear any more can be changed into new items.

You can take things away:

Shorten skirts, tops and trousers

Shorten sleeves

Change collars

You can add things:

Patterns

Pleats

Length

Activity sheet – Recycling

Reuse (2)

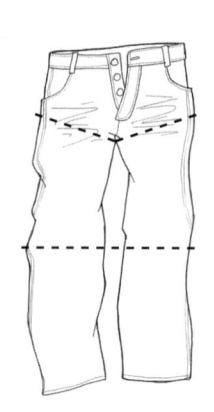

The fabric from clothes can be reused to make a bag. For example, one pair of jeans can be made into five bags.

☞ 1 Look at the diagram on the right to see how to cut jeans up. Cut up a pair of jeans so you have five pieces of material. Choose one piece and design your bag below.

1 Add a seam to make a bag.	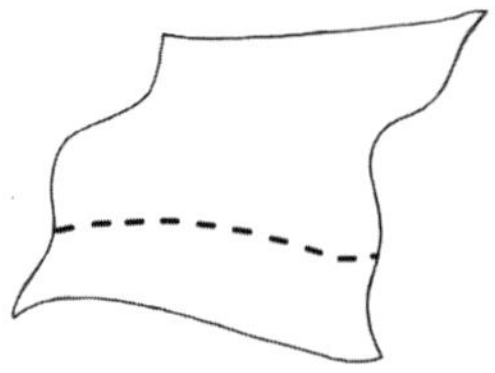	
2 Add a design.	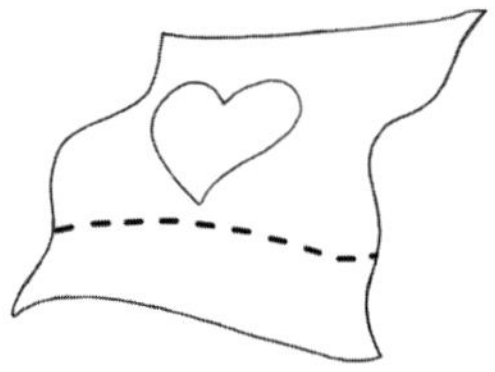	
3 Add a handle.		
4 Add a fastening.		

☞ 2 Once you are happy with your design, make your bag.

28   Textiles 2   © Folens (copiable page)

Teacher's notes

Adding colour to fabric

Objectives

- To be able to name and describe four different methods of adding colour to fabric from four different countries
- To know how to complete four methods of adding colour to fabric
- To understand that some traditional techniques are adapted and used on a commercial scale

Prior knowledge

Students need to know that there are numerous ways that colour can be added to textiles. They need to know that dyes are used to colour threads and yarns as well as the fabric itself.

NC links

Key concepts: 1.1 Designing and making; 1.2 Cultural understanding; 1.3 Creativity
Key processes: c, d, e, f
Range and content: a, e, j, k
Curriculum opportunities: a, b, e

Northern Ireland PoS

Designing: c, g
Manufacturing: d

Scottish attainment targets

Processes and how they are applied: Level D

Welsh PoS

Skills: Designing: 2, 4
Skills: Making: 1, 2, 12

Background

This unit looks at a wide range of ways that colour is added to fabrics from different parts of the globe. The different methods of adding colour have been selected to illustrate that fabrics can be dyed or can have additional threads of fabrics added to decorate them.

Starter activity

The world map from the Resource sheet, 'Where in the world?', indicates where four techniques have originated and could be displayed on a whiteboard or a wall.

Students could guess how they think the techniques work and then revisit their answers on completion of the unit. Were they correct?

Resource sheets and Activity sheets

The Activity sheet, 'Shisha work', describes how to complete shisha work. Students will need to be shown how to complete this and will need time to practise the technique to achieve quality results.

The Activity sheet, 'Shibori dyeing', requires some practical resources for students to use. The fabric dyes should be placed into spill-proof paint containers. Students need to wear protective clothing whilst they are working with the dye. There must be plenty of space to dry the fabric once it has been dyed.

The Activity sheet, 'Jacquard or Fair Isle patterns for knitted fabrics', illustrates how patterns are generated when a fabric has been knitted. This activity enables students to see that patterns and designs are generated from small blocks of colour, which each represent a stitch in the construction of the patterned knitted fabric. Students can create their own designs on the sheet.

The Activity sheet, 'Creating a checked fabric', requires students to have some resources to create their own checked fabric.

Plenary

Place each student's name into a bag at the start of the lesson. At the end of the lesson one or two names are pulled out of the bag. The student describes the technique they have learnt, or the two students alternately describe how to complete the technique.

Students could show their examples of the finished technique and a discussion generated: where on the textile product/garment could the technique be used? Why might the technique be most suitable?

Resource sheet – Adding colour to fabric

Where in the world?

This world map shows where different techniques of adding colour to fabrics originate from.

Fair Isle: knitted items using limited colours, for example, two colours per row

Scotland: woven fabric (tartan)

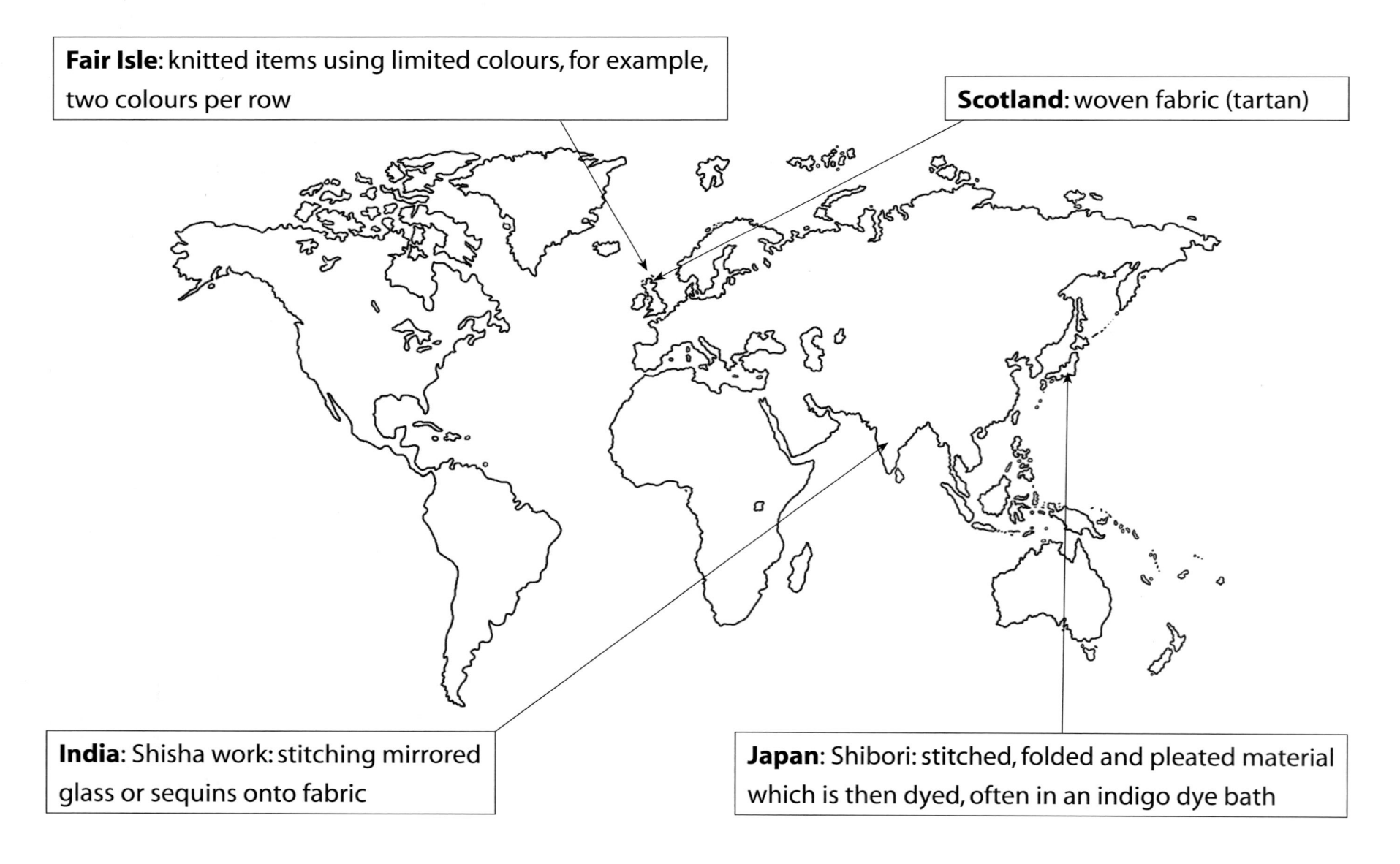

Japan: Shibori: stitched, folded and pleated material which is then dyed, often in an indigo dye bath

India: Shisha work: stitching mirrored glass or sequins onto fabric

Activity sheet – Adding colour to fabric

Shisha work

In India, textiles are decorated with pieces of mirror that are stitched into place.

☞ Try creating your own piece of shisha work.

You will need:

- A piece of plain fabric such as calico
- Perle or soft thread
- A small circular piece of mirrored acrylic
- A large-eyed needle

	Start stitching the mirror in place like this.
	These stitches hold the mirror in place.
	Stitch until the mirror is firmly in position.
	A row of buttonhole stitching is used to create a 'ring' around the mirror.
	The buttonhole stitching must carry on all around the mirror.
	This is the finished shisha mirror in place.

© Folens (copiable page)   Textiles 2

Activity sheet – Adding colour to fabric

Shibori dyeing

Shibori is a Japanese tie-dyeing technique. This technique uses fabrics made from natural fibres as they absorb dye easily. For example, fabrics made from silk or cotton.

☞ Try creating your own piece of shibori dyeing.

You will need:

- A dowel rod, plastic bottle or plastic drainpipe
- A piece of natural fabric such as silk or a fine cotton fabric
- A needle
- Thread or string
- Liquid dyes
- A paintbrush

	Twist, pleat or fold the fabric and wrap it around the dowel rod.
	The dowel rod should be covered in fabric, leaving the ends free so you can hold it.
	Stitch or tie the fabric in place around the dowel rod.
	Ensure the fabric is wet.
	Paint the dye onto the fabric. Use several colours at once for the best effect.
	Dry and untie the finished fabric to show the shibori pattern.

Activity sheet – Adding colour to fabric

Jacquard or Fair Isle patterns for knitted fabrics

☞ 1 Design a pattern for a knitted fabric. The list below gives some tips to get you started.

- Designs for knitted fabrics are created on a grid.
- Each square represents a stitch.
- There may be more than two colours on a row.
- The more colours used on a row the more complex the pattern.

☞ 2 Colour the squares in the grid below to create your own Jacquard/Fair Isle pattern. The diagram on the left should give you some ideas. Your pattern could be based on stars, leaves, snowflakes, rectangles, triangles or flowers for example.

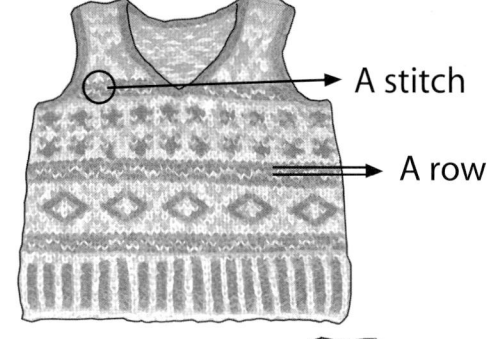

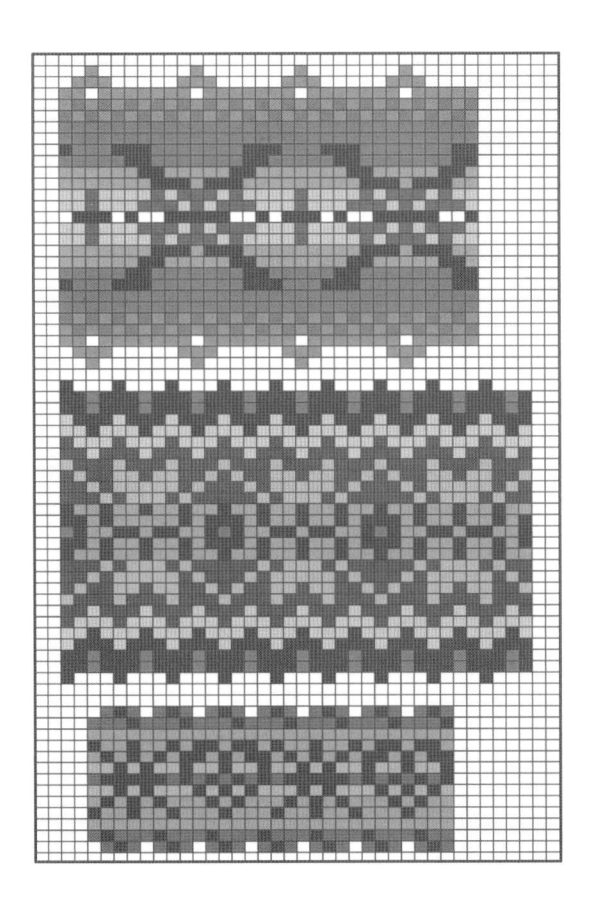

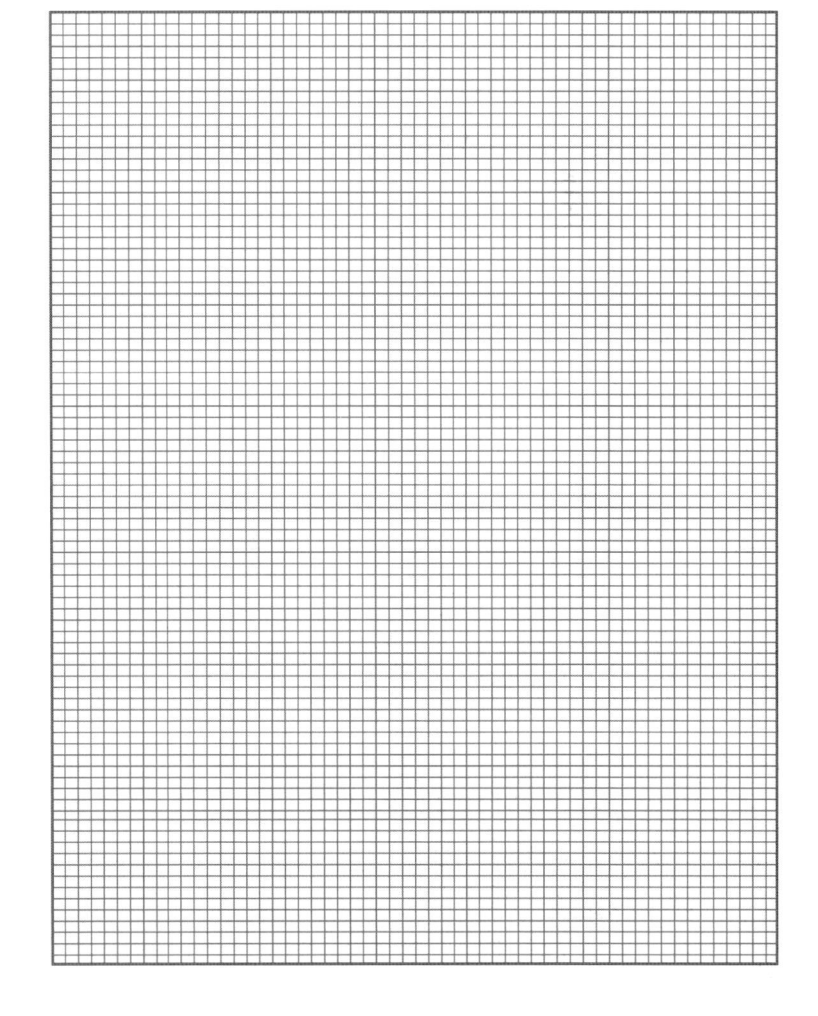

© Folens (copiable page)   Textiles 2

Activity sheet – Adding colour to fabric

Creating a checked fabric

☞ Try creating your own piece of checked fabric.

You will need:

- A rectangle of strong card
- A bodkin
- Scissors
- Sticky tape
- Different coloured yarns

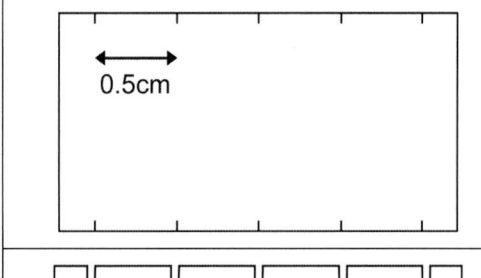	Measure and mark every 0.5cm at each side of the card. Make sure the marks are opposite each other.
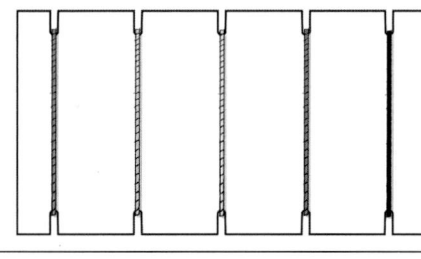	Cut slots in the card at both sides. Wind the yarn up and down the card.
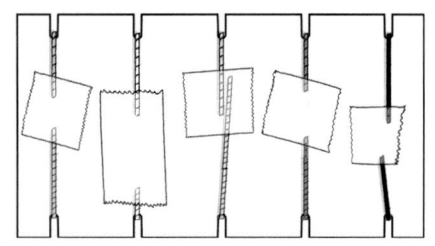	Secure the yarn using sticky tape.
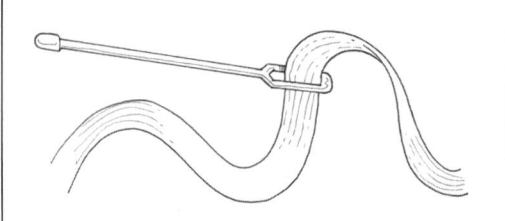	Thread the bodkin with yarn.
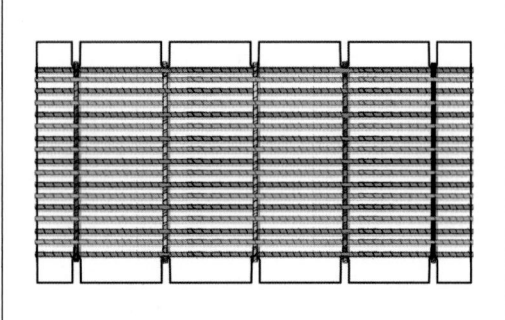	Weave yarn over and under the threads across the card. Repeat the weaving action, until you have filled up the card. Change the colour of the yarn you weave across the card. You should see different coloured squares or 'checks' being formed.

Teacher's notes

Smart and technical fabrics

Objectives

- To understand the terms 'smart' and 'technical' fabrics
- To understand how products made from smart and technical fabrics make life easier
- To be able to describe the term 'microfibre'
- To become more discerning consumers

Prior knowledge

Students need to know how fabrics are constructed. Students should understand the term 'fibre', how important a fibre is in the construction of a fabric and that fabrics behave very differently because of the way they have been made.

NC links

Key concepts: 1.1 Designing and making
Key processes: b, c
Range and content: a, b, d, e, l
Curriculum opportunities: a, b, c, e

Northern Ireland PoS

Manufacturing materials, components, techniques and processes
Designing: h

Scottish attainment targets

Needs and how they are met: Level D

Welsh PoS

Skills: Making: 14

Background

This unit looks at how smart and technical fabrics differ, as well as how these fabrics can make our lives easier. It covers case studies of products that use these smart and technical fabrics. The Activity sheets allow students to explore these fabrics.

Starter activity

Use the case studies on the Resource sheet, 'Textile products and smart fabrics', to create a set of cards. Ask students to study these products and place them into rank order, for example, which product could make their life easier? Which product do they think is the most expensive? Which product is the least useful? Which product do they like the most?

Display two T-shirts with price labels: one a cotton, value T-shirt; the other should be made from a more technical fabric, for example, a football, rugby or tennis shirt. Ask students to think about which T-shirt they would purchase and why, and ask them to consider the function and cost of the shirts.

Resource sheets and Activity sheets

The Resource sheet, 'Technical fabrics and microfibres', explains to students the more technical fabrics that are manufactured to perform specific functions. This sheet also looks at the wicking process.

The Activity sheet, 'The use of smart and technical fabrics', requires students to think about how these products impact on our everyday lives.

The Activity sheet, 'Smart and technical fabrics... what am I?', is designed to get students thinking about the functions of technical fabrics and to consider how they affect our everyday lives.

The Activity sheet, 'Analysing a product', is designed to increase students' analytical skills so they become more discerning consumers. Students have to complete the product analysis chart about various case study products.

Plenary

A design extension activity could be to consider developing the case study products from the Resource sheet, 'Textile products and smart fabrics'. How could the products be improved? What parts of the products could be changed to improve them for different consumers, the same consumer, or how could the technical function be used for another purpose?

Resource sheet – Smart and technical fabrics

Textile products and smart fabrics

A smart fabric will sense changes around you. To create a smart fabric, sensors are woven into the material. Smart fabrics are made into garments or products to make life easier.

Smart fabric
Sensors are woven into the fabric.

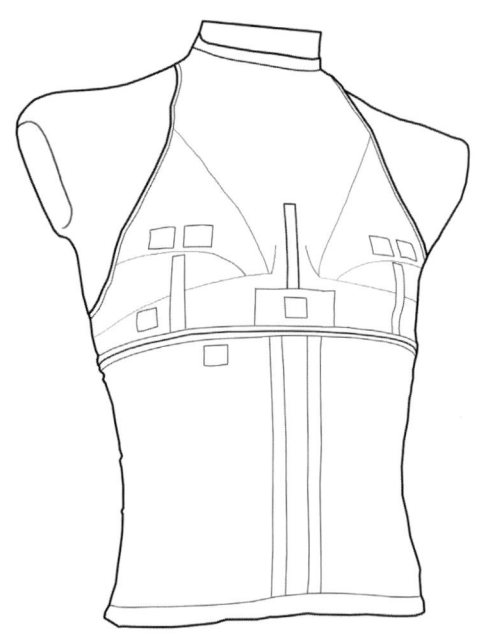

The Wi-Fi detector shirt
The shirt will change colour when it picks up a Wi-Fi signal.

Puddlejumper raincoat
The raincoat lights up when rain hits the sensors.

MP3 jacket
Anyone wearing the jacket can control their MP3 player by touching the fabric switches on the sleeve.

Resource sheet – Smart and technical fabrics

Technical fabrics and microfibres

Technical fabrics are often made from microfibres. Microfibres are ten times finer than a human hair. Technical fabrics help to make our lives comfortable or easier.

Some fabrics have a coating that kills bacteria. This coating is called **antibacterial**. It makes the fabric technical.

Microfibres can be made with a hollow core. The core can be filled with substances like creams or perfumes. This is known as **microencapsulation**. The substances are released slowly. For example, this wrist band is filled with an insect repellent.

Coolmax® is a fabric made from microfibres. Coolmax® can absorb and evaporate perspiration easily. This process is known as **wicking**. Shirts made from this are often used in sport.

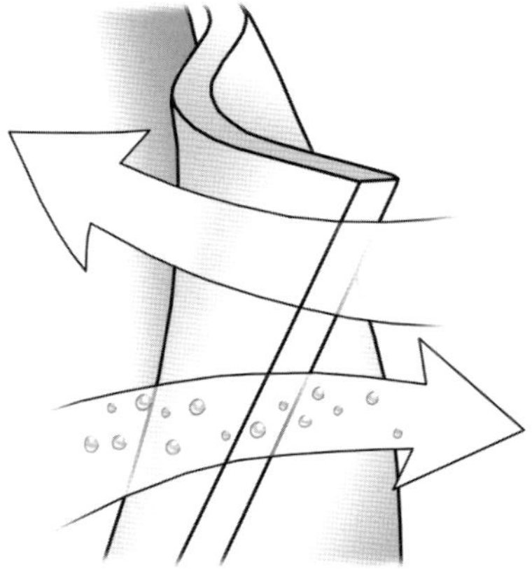

© Folens (copiable page)   Textiles 2

Activity sheet – Smart and technical fabrics

The use of smart and technical fabrics

☞ 1 Cut out the cards.

DuPont™ Kevlar® fabrics	**Antibacterial coating**
DuPont™ Nomex® fabrics	**Mylar fabric**

☞ 2 Rank the products:

- as to how much easier they make our lives
- as to how much safer they make our lives
- according to the cost (high, medium or low cost).

Activity sheet – Smart and technical fabrics

Smart and technical fabrics… what am I?

☞ Use the information on the Resource sheet, 'Technical fabrics and microfibres', to help you work out what fabric I am. The first one has been done to help you.

What fabric am I?

- I am used to make protective clothing.
- I am worn to help prevent injury.
- I am rather expensive.

I am *Kevlar*

What special coating am I?

- I am used to make protective clothing.
- I am worn in a hospital operating theatre or a laboratory.
- I am rather expensive.

I am _____

What fabric am I?

- I am used to make sports clothing.
- I am worn when exercising.
- I help to keep the body at the correct temperature.

I am _____

What fabric am I?

- I am used to make protective fireproof clothing.
- I am worn on a racing track, for example, at go-karting or Formula One.
- I am very expensive.

I am _____

© Folens (copiable page)   Textiles 2   39

Activity sheet – Smart and technical fabrics

Analysing a product

☞ Choose two smart fabric products and draw an example of each. Explain what they do and how they make life easier. Use the word bank to help you. Give each product a star rating (* = useless, ** = OK, *** = very useful). An example has been given.

Product	What does the product do?	How will it make life easier?	Star rating	How could it be better?
MP3 jacket	It allows the wearer to use an MP3 player at any time and in any place.	It means you can listen to music or access the Internet at any time.	* (**) ***	The jacket could be made more suitable for girls by making it less straight lined.
			* ** ***	
			* ** ***	

Word bank

- Rain
- Seen
- Reflect
- Saves time
- Cool
- Easier
- Convenient
- Size
- Style
- Shape

Teacher's notes

Industrial practice

Objectives

- To be able to calculate the cost of a simple product
- To know that there are hidden costs in the manufacturing of items such as heating, lighting and rent
- To have a comprehensive understanding of the terminology used when making a product

Prior knowledge

Students need to know about seams and components such as zips, buttons, press studs, poppers, and so on. They would also benefit from having some understanding of the language used in industrial manufacturing, for example, prototype, specification and quality assurance (QA).

NC links

Key concepts: 1.1 Designing and making
Key processes: e, f
Range and content: a, j, m
Curriculum opportunities: a, b, c, e

Northern Ireland PoS

Designing: b, c

Scottish attainment targets

Resources and how they are managed: Level C
Processes and how they are applied: Level D

Welsh PoS

Skills: Designing: 2, 4
Skills: Making: 2, 10

Background

This unit looks at concepts related to the industrial manufacture of textile products. There are two Resource sheets to help explain the production of textile items on a commercial scale. The Activity sheets are focused on activities that are completed in industry.

Starter activity

Each student should be asked to focus on their own pencil case. Ask them what would be needed by the company who made them, for example, sewing machines, materials, zips, fabrics, decorative components, and so on. Try to get students to think about where the product is made and any costs involved such as rent of a factory and the cost of heating and lighting. This will help them to consider all the elements required to make a product.

Resource sheets and Activity sheets

The Resource sheet, 'Clothing manufacture', is a diagram to help clarify the different departments in a company and their role.

The Resource sheet, 'One-off, batch and mass production', provides a glossary of terms.

The Activity sheet, 'Costing products', is about how to price a product. Students are asked to consider the hidden costs in the production of a product. Some students may need some one-to-one support for this task; alternatively this could be completed as a group. The calculations get harder further down the chart.

The Activity sheet, 'Product analysis', is about analysing an existing product and adapting and developing it to create a 'new' product. Students are to create new designs for a passport holder. Students must be asked to consider the consumer when designing a new product.

The Activity sheet, 'Making identical products', allows students to create a detailed product specification from a sketch of a shopping bag. They are introduced to quality assurance (QA) – the system industry uses to ensure all products are identical and meet the industry standards.

Plenary

The top line of boxes from the Resource sheet, 'Clothing manufacture', can provide cards for the plenary activity. The cards should be placed face down on a table for a student to select one. The rest of the class ask the student holding the card questions to find out what the word on the card is. The student can only respond 'yes' or 'no' to any questions asked. Additional cards could be added if students have completed the other Activity sheets, 'Costing products' or 'Making identical products'. Once the class has guessed the word on the card then the student holding it should explain the term to the class.

Resource sheet – Industrial practice

Clothing manufacture

Design → Develop the range of products:
- Design products
- Final design ideas
- Pattern making

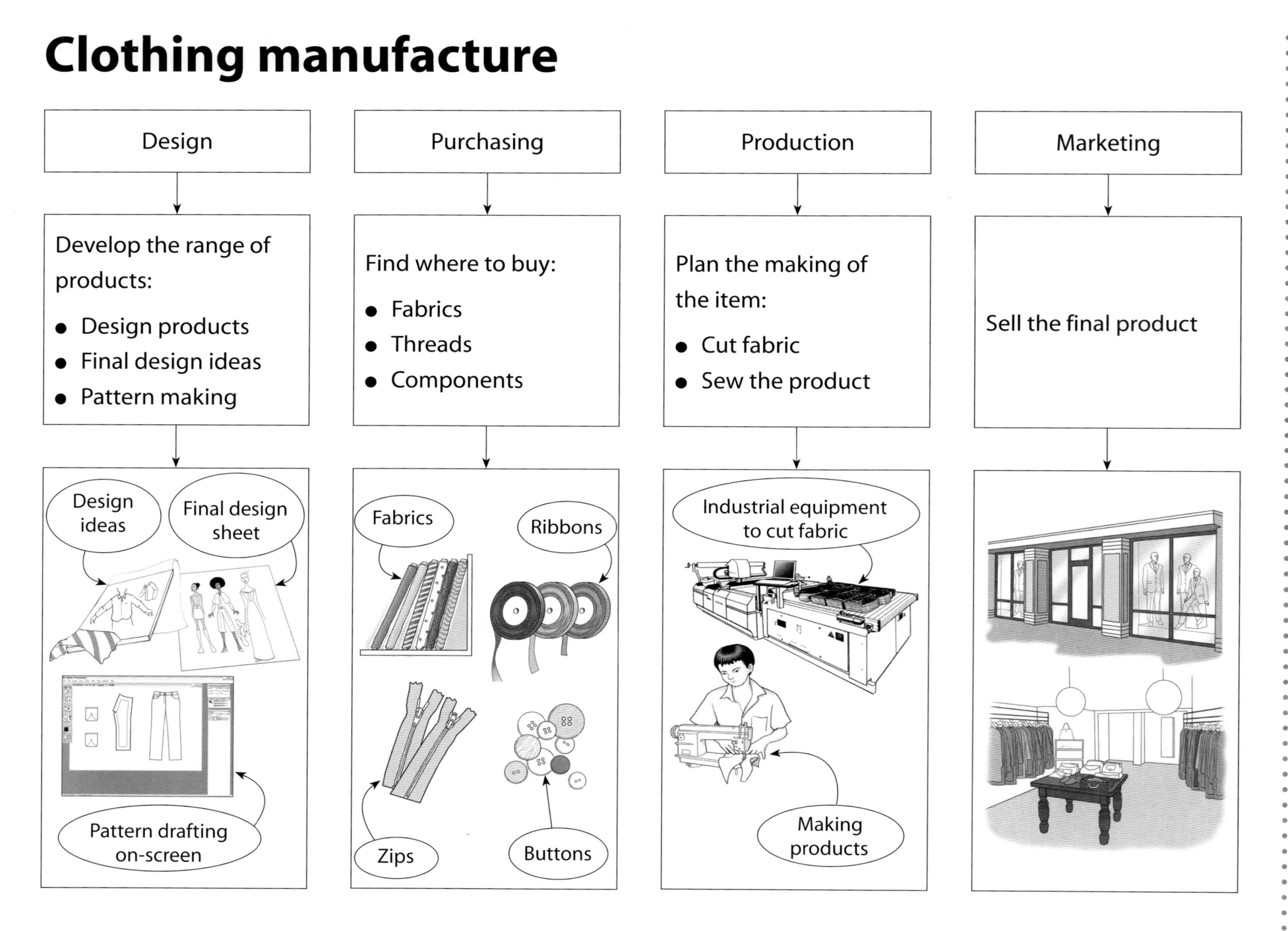

→ Final design sheet / Design ideas / Pattern drafting on-screen

Purchasing → Find where to buy:
- Fabrics
- Threads
- Components

→ Ribbons / Buttons / Fabrics / Zips

Production → Plan the making of the item:
- Cut fabric
- Sew the product

→ Industrial equipment to cut fabric / Making products

Marketing → Sell the final product

Resource sheet – Industrial practice

One-off, batch and mass production

Textile products are made in different amounts depending on their use and function.

Batch production
A limited number of identical products are made. Many textile products are made in limited numbers to avoid lots of people having identical items. For example, a designer hooded jacket or a football team's kit.

One-off
Only one product is made. It could be for a special occasion or simply for a person to have a unique item. For example, a prom dress or a made-to-measure bespoke suit.

Mass production
A large number of the same products are continuously produced. These are products that are constantly in high demand. For example, jeans and bed sheets.

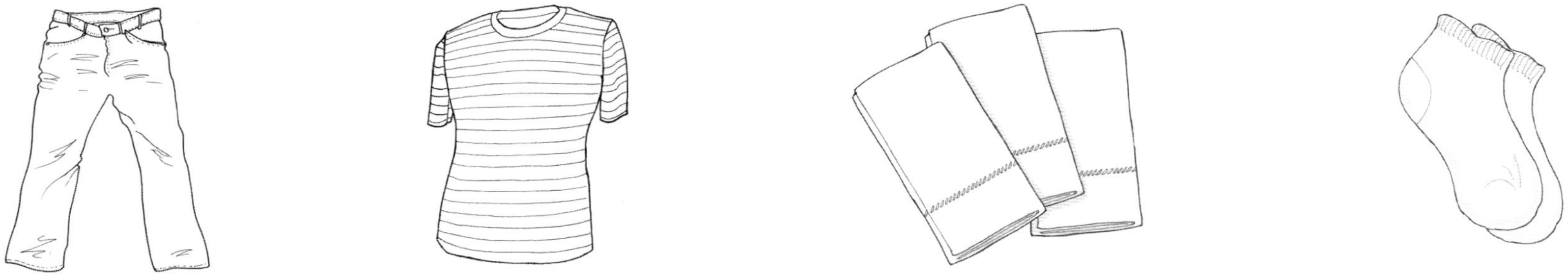

© Folens (copiable page)   Textiles 2

Activity sheet – Industrial practice

Costing products

To make money (a profit), a company must work out how much it costs to make a product to start with. A company has to sell a product for more than it costs to make, to make a profit.

☞ 1 Use the chart below to work out how much it will cost to make a pencil case.

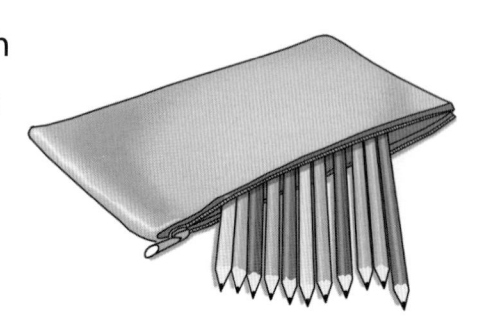

Item	Cost	Amount needed	Actual cost
Fabric	£4 per metre 100cm wide (fabric bought in 10cm lengths)	2 x 20cm x 15cm (1 x 10cm strip costs 40p, 2 x 40p = 80p)	80p
Labour	£4.50 per hour	30 minutes	
Rent and rates on the factory space	£24 per day (24 hours)	30 minutes	
Cost of electricity and water	£12 per day (24 hours)	30 minutes	
Thread	£1.60 per reel (1000 metres a reel)	100 metres	

☞ 2 To work out the selling price of the pencil case, you need to add a mark-up, for example 20p, so you can make a profit. Use the chart below to help work out the selling price of the pencil case.

Item	Cost
Cost of making one pencil case	
20 per cent mark-up	
	Total cost:

Activity sheet – Industrial practice

Product analysis

The design industry looks at existing products to help them design new products.

☞ 1 Look closely at the passport holder. Answer the questions below. Use the word bank to help you.

What does the product do?	
Who has the product been designed for?	
What is the product made from?	
What are its good points?	
What are its bad points?	

Word bank

- Protect
- Stiff
- Style
- Hold
- Cover
- New
- Clean
- Colour
- Leather
- Plastic
- Man
- Woman

☞ 2 How could you make this product better? Sketch three 'new' passport holders.

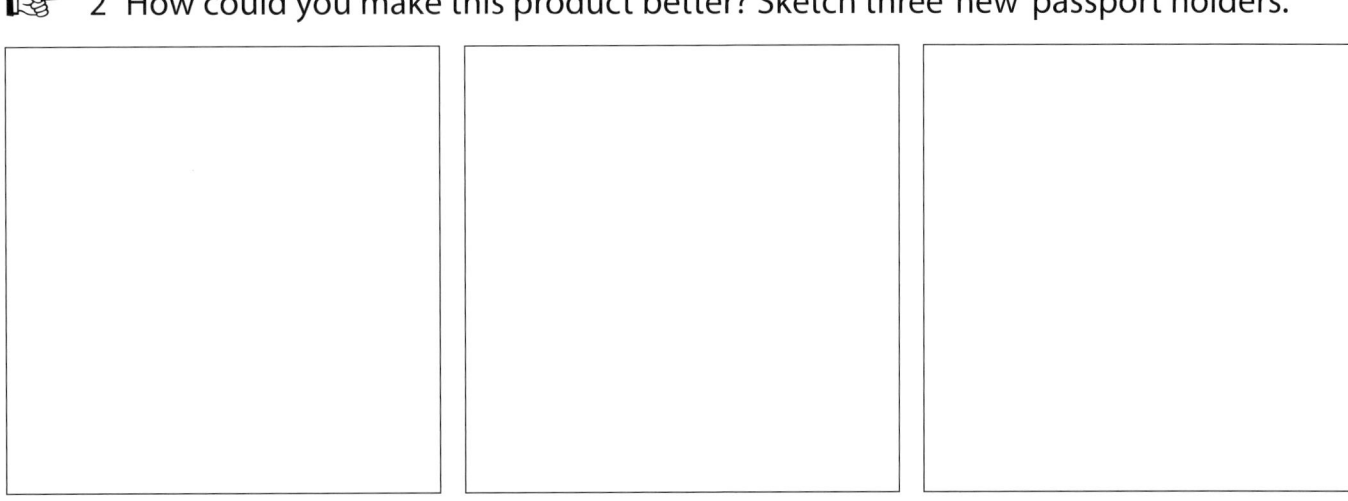

Add something to it.	Change something about it.	Adapt it to do something else.

© Folens (copiable page)   Textiles 2   45

Activity sheet – Industrial practice

Making identical products

The design industry has to make products that are the same every time. Important information about the product has to be recorded so that other people can make it in the same way. This is known as a **product specification**. **Quality assurance** is the process that ensures all products are made to the same high standard.

☞ 1 Produce a product specification for an eco-shopping bag. Use the information below to help you complete the rest of the sheet.

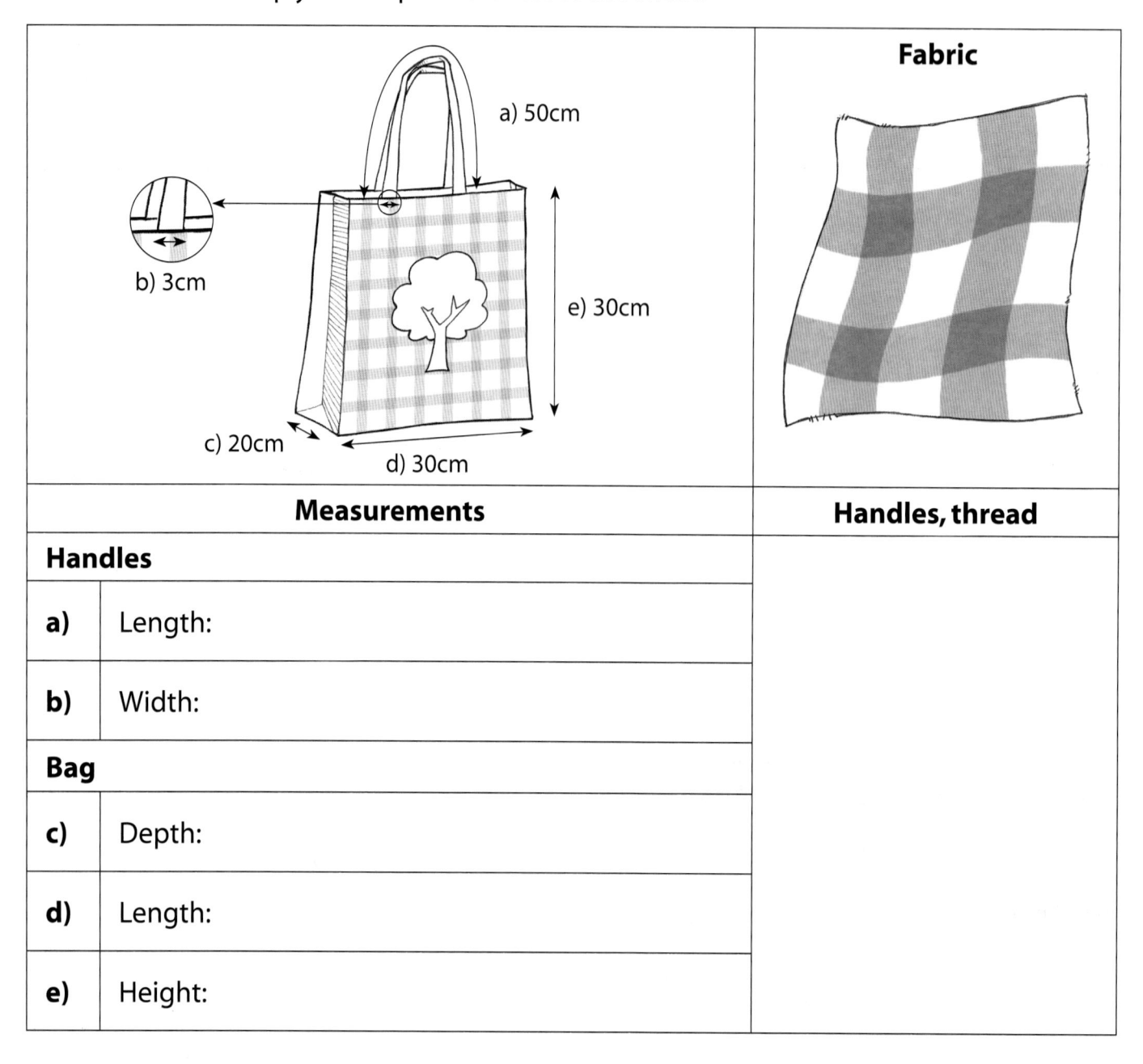

		Measurements	Fabric
			Handles, thread
Handles			
a)	Length:		
b)	Width:		
Bag			
c)	Depth:		
d)	Length:		
e)	Height:		

Bag diagram measurements:
- a) 50cm
- b) 3cm
- c) 20cm
- d) 30cm
- e) 30cm

☞ 2 Why do you think this product specification would help to make lots of eco-shopping bags that are the same?

Teacher's notes

Aesthetics

Objectives
- To look at the use of textiles as a means to enhance the aesthetics of a product
- To learn some methods of using textiles for decoration

Prior knowledge
Students should know about the use of ready-made textile decoration such as lace, ribbon and motifs. Students should also be able to use simple hand sewing techniques.

NC links
Key concepts: 1.1 Designing and making; 1.2 Cultural understanding; 1.3 Creativity
Key processes: e, f
Range and content: a, e, j
Curriculum opportunities: a, b

Northern Ireland PoS
Manufacturing materials, components, techniques and processes

Scottish attainment targets
Processes and how they are applied: Level B, Level C

Welsh PoS
Skills: Designing: 1, 2, 3, 8
Skills: Making: 12

Background
This unit looks at some less common ways of decorating textile products and of using textiles to do this. Further information on the art of braiding can be found on the Internet or see *Beginner's Guide to Braiding: The Craft of Kumihimo* by Jacqui Carey (Search Press). Rest assured this technique is quite simple to learn and surprisingly therapeutic! Any wool or thicker thread can be used – decorative wools give more interesting braids but may be more difficult to handle to start with.

Starter activity
Students could look at a plain garment and discuss ways in which it might be decorated or embellished. They should discuss the possibilities of 'temporary' embellishments that could be removed when desired, and of more permanent decoration. They could look at some historical uses of embellishment such as a range of pictures of hats or corsages from history, and then discuss how styles of embellishment have changed.

Resource sheets and Activity sheets
The Resource sheet, 'Braiding', gives an introduction to braiding that can then be tried using the Activity sheet, 'Make a braid'. This activity works well in small groups, or with students working independently.

The Activity sheet, 'Making a fabric brooch', shows students how to make a brooch using a flower design. It then gives them the opportunity to design and make their own brooch. This activity could be carried out individually or in small groups.

The Activity sheet, 'Couching', shows students how to decorate a piece of fabric by sewing cord, strings of beads or sequins to it.

Plenary
Students could compare and evaluate their own and others' work and could rate the difficulty and aesthetic quality of each activity.

Follow-up or extension activities could include looking at a wider range of ways to make fabric jewellery, for example, winding dyed silk ribbon around plastic bangles or bobbin knitting with elastic to make bracelets and rings. You could also look at the use of pom-poms to decorate belts and hats. This could provide a good enterprise activity for students.

© Folens · Textiles 2

Resource sheet – Aesthetics

Braiding

Braiding is a very old craft from Japan where it is called Kumihimo. Braiding has many uses but was traditionally used as part of the Samurai Warriors' armour.

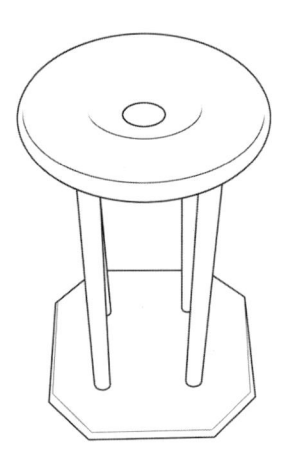

Braiding is used for belts, curtain tie-backs, bag handles and other decorative things. It is traditionally completed on a round stand called a marudai. Marudais are usually made from wood.

To use a marudai you will need eight bobbins and a small bag filled with an equal weight of pennies.

1. Wind all the bobbins with the same long length of wool. Leave a 30cm end and fasten the bobbin with an elastic band so it doesn't unwind.

2. When you have wound all eight bobbins tie the long ends together.

3. Tie the bag of pennies to the knot. Drop the bag through the hole in the top of the marudai.

4. Arrange the bobbins in pairs. Adjust the length of the bobbins so that neither the bag of pennies nor the bobbins touch the ground.

5. As you work, the bag of pennies will keep reaching the ground. When it does you will need to tie it further up the braid to keep your braid even.

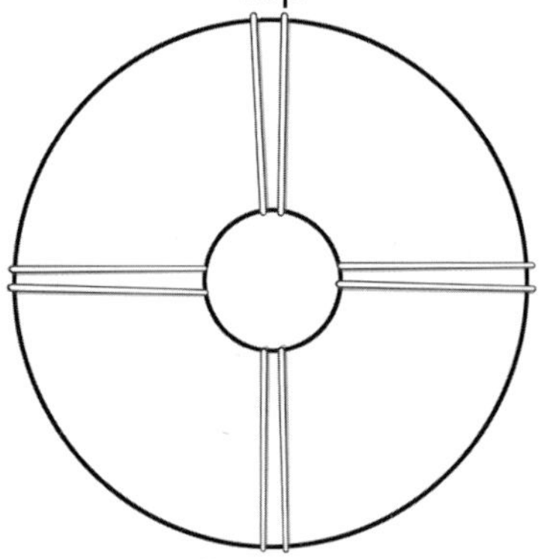

To start making your braid, follow the instructions on the Activity sheet, 'Make a braid'.

When your braid is the right length, or you have used up all the wool, sew the ends together to stop them unravelling and neatly trim the end.

You could try different wools, embroidery threads or ribbons to make different textured braids.

Activity sheet – Aesthetics

Make a braid

Make your own round braid.

☞ Put the marudai on the floor in front of you and kneel or sit on a cushion to work. Follow these four moves:

Move 1

Lift the two threads from the bottom and put them down between the two at the top.

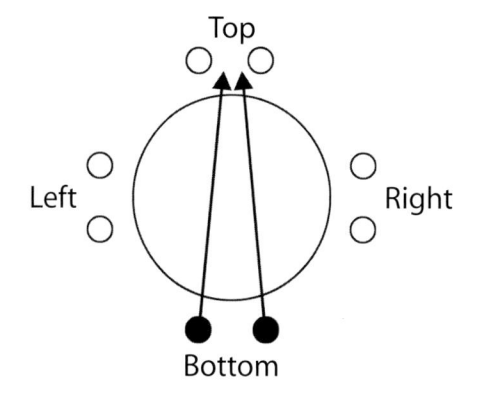

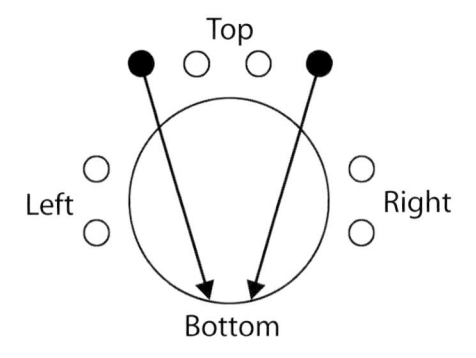

Move 2

Lift the two outer threads from the top and move them to the bottom.

Move 3

Lift the two threads from the right and put them down between the two on the left.

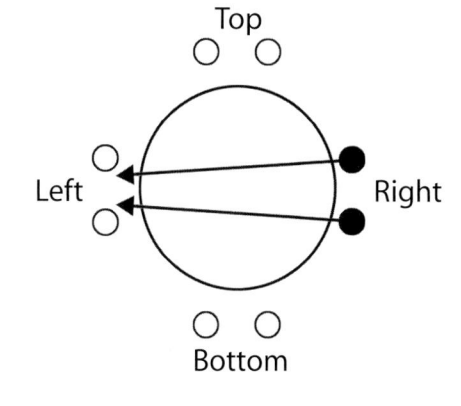

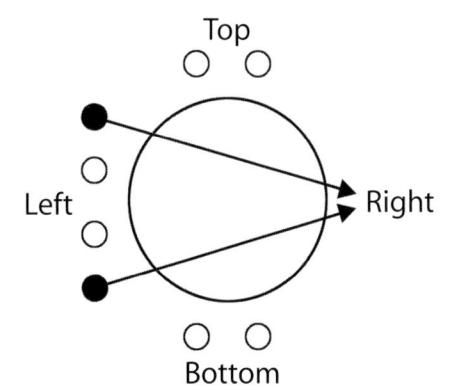

Move 4

Lift the two outer threads from the left and move them to the right.

Repeat these moves until your braid is finished.

© Folens (copiable page)   Textiles 2   49

Activity sheet – Aesthetics

Making a fabric brooch

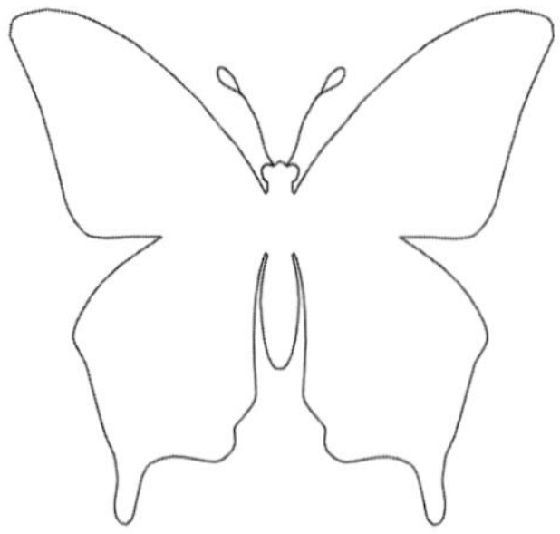

☞ 1 Make a fabric brooch.

You will need:

- Two colours of felt for the petals
- Green felt for the leaves
- A button
- Brightly coloured sewing thread
- A needle
- A brooch pin

1 Cut a flower shape out of each of the coloured felts.

2 Cut one or two leaf shapes out of the green felt.

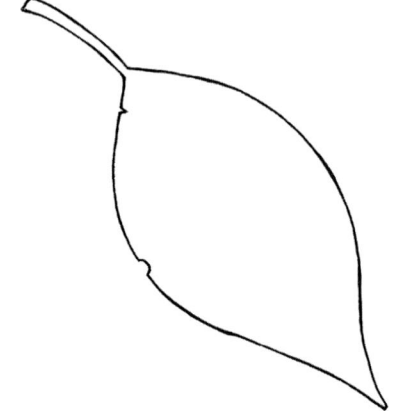

3 Place the shapes on top of each other.

Sew up through the button and back down through all the layers.

Do this several times to make sure everything is secure.

Now sew on the brooch pin.

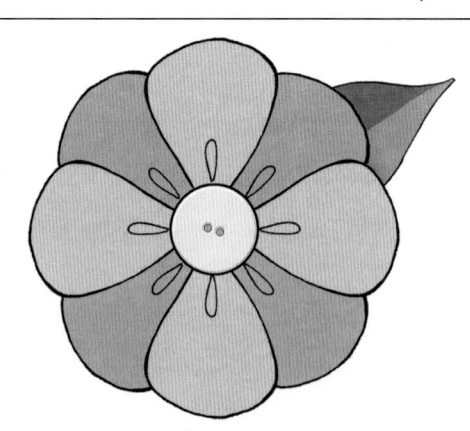

☞ 2 You could now make a butterfly brooch or create your own brooch design.

50   Textiles 2   © Folens (copiable page)

Activity sheet – Aesthetics

Couching

Couching is a way of decorating fabric by sewing strings of beads, sequins or cord onto it. Couching is often used to decorate cuffs, hems and collars.

☞ Use couching to decorate a piece of fabric with any design you like.

You will need:

- A piece of plain fabric
- A pencil
- A needle and thread
- Coloured cord
- Pins

1 Choose a piece of plain fabric and a length of cord.	
2 Use a pencil to lightly draw a pattern onto the fabric.	
3 Lay the cord along your pattern and pin it into place.	
4 Sew the cord to the fabric. Each stitch should start on one side of the cord and finish on the other.	
5 Sew all the way along the cord. Then remove the pins.	

© Folens (copiable page)   Textiles 2   51

Teacher's notes

Accessories

Objectives
- To be able to identify the function of a textile product
- To develop analytical skills so students can evaluate their own designs against a set of criteria

Prior knowledge
Students should know what an accessory is. They should also understand vocabulary like 'functional', 'criteria' and 'appearance'.

NC links
Key concepts: 1.1 Designing and making
Key processes: a, b, c, d
Range and content: a, b, e, j, k, l, m
Curriculum opportunities: a, b, c, e

Northern Ireland PoS
Designing: c, f, g, h

Scottish attainment targets
Reviewing and reporting on tasks: Level D

Welsh PoS
Skills: Designing: 2, 8, 9
Skills: Making: 10

Background

This unit looks at a wide range of textile accessories that are part of our everyday lives. It explores how some accessories make homes or outfits look better, and how some accessories help to keep us safe and have a practical function.

Starter activity

Place an accessory in a bag but don't let students see what it is. Students are only allowed to see and/or feel the bag to try and guess what the accessory is. They can ask questions to which you can only answer 'yes' or 'no'. Students should guess the accessory and who might use it. This could be completed as a class or group activity.

One of the accessories could be used as a starting point for designing a new product. Students could produce the specification for the accessory and then create a new design for a product with the same function.

Resource sheets and Activity sheets

The Resource sheet, 'What is an accessory?', illustrates the wide range of textile accessories we are familiar with in our everyday lives. This sheet will raise students' awareness of the range and various functions of textile accessories. It should help them to understand that products need to fulfil a function when they are being designed.

The Activity sheet, 'Hats and their functions', will teach students to identify the function of a textile accessory. This analytical skill should be transferred to the students' design work. Students should be able to think about the function of a specific product when they are in the process of developing the design idea.

The Activity sheet, 'Accessories for sport', indicates to students that there are a number of different accessories that can help us participate in a wide range of sports. Here students match the accessory to the sport to help them consider the function of the accessory.

The Activity sheet, 'Designing a cushion cover', guides students through a strategy to design a cushion for students to use in a room at home.

The Activity sheet, 'Eco-friendly bags', is about getting students to consider a series of bags. Students look at the picture cards carefully and rank them according to the criteria given. They are also asked to talk through their ranking decisions with a partner. This will encourage students to verbalize their decisions.

Plenary

Students should now have a better understanding of what an accessory is and what the function of an accessory might be.

Take ten cards with either the word 'accessory' or 'function' written on them. Fan out the cards and ask students to select a card. Students need to name an accessory or a function depending on the word on the card and then ask the person closest to them to provide the additional information, either the function or the name of the accessory – the opposite to what was on the card.

Resource sheet – Accessories

What is an accessory?

Accessories can be worn to make outfits look more attractive or to make our homes look nice. They can also be used to keep you safe, warm or cool, as well as to make life easier.

Accessories worn with outfits

- Jewellery
- Scarves
- Bags
- Hats
- Ties
- Gloves

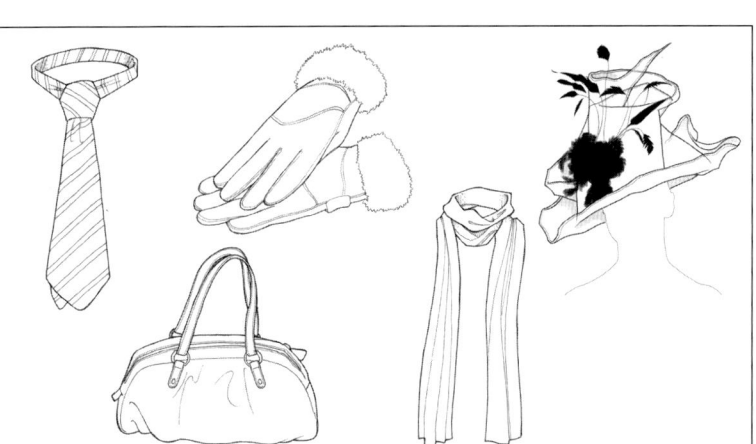

Accessories for the home

- Cushions
- Towels
- Tea towels
- Curtains
- Bean bags

Accessories to keep you safe

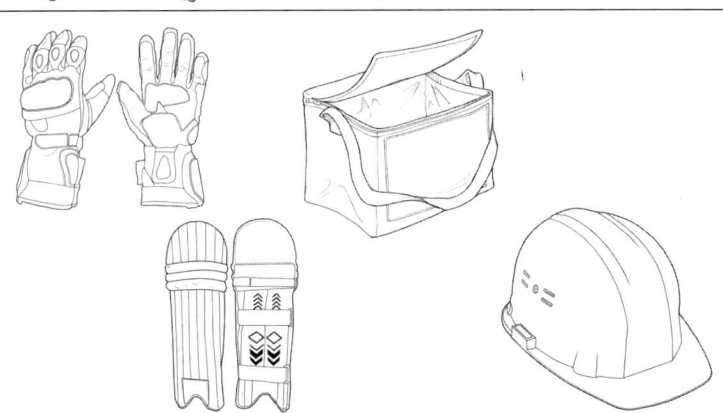

- Hard hats
- Cool bags
- Gloves
- Cricket pads

Accessories to make life easier

- Rucksacks
- Wash bags
- Camera bags
- Shopping bags

© Folens (copiable page)   Textiles 2   53

Activity sheet – Accessories

Hats and their functions

☞ Use the word banks to help you complete the chart below. The first one has been done for you.

Hat	Function	Occasion
A chef's hat	Safety and hygiene	Preparing and serving food
A builder's hard hat		
A beanie hat		
A wedding hat		
A ski hat		
A novelty hat		

Function word bank
- Warm
- Appearance
- Protection
- Cool
- Costume

Occasions word bank
- Wedding
- Summer holiday
- Everyday
- Leisure
- Carnival
- Celebration
- Work
- Festival

54   Textiles 2   © Folens (copiable page)

Activity sheet – Accessories

Accessories for sport

☞ Match the accessory to the sport by drawing arrows. Some accessories can be used for more than one sport.

Accessory	Sport
Swimming hat	Golf
Cricket bag	Walking
Sun visor	Skateboarding
Boot bag	Tennis
Kneepads	Cricket
Golf club covers	Squash or badminton
Warm hat	Swimming
Sweat bands	Snowboarding

© Folens (copiable page)   Textiles 2

Activity sheet – Accessories

Designing a cushion cover

☞ Design a cushion to use in a room at home. Choose one idea from each column. Draw lines from each of your choices and use them to help design your cushion.

Shape	Colours	Theme	Adding colour	Fastening	Position of opening
Rectangle	Tropical →	→ Flowers →	→ Appliqué	Zip	Across the back
Square	Earthy	Triangles	Hand-stitching	Velcro	Over an edge
Circle	Watery	Squares	Machine-stitching	Flap	

Your cushion could look a bit like this:

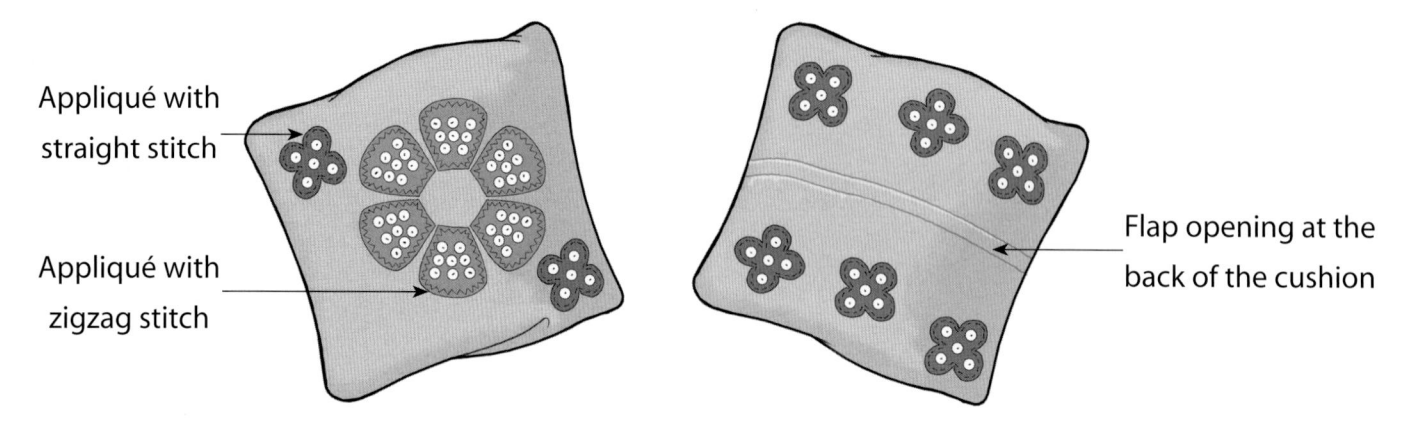

Appliqué with straight stitch

Appliqué with zigzag stitch

Flap opening at the back of the cushion

Front of cushion

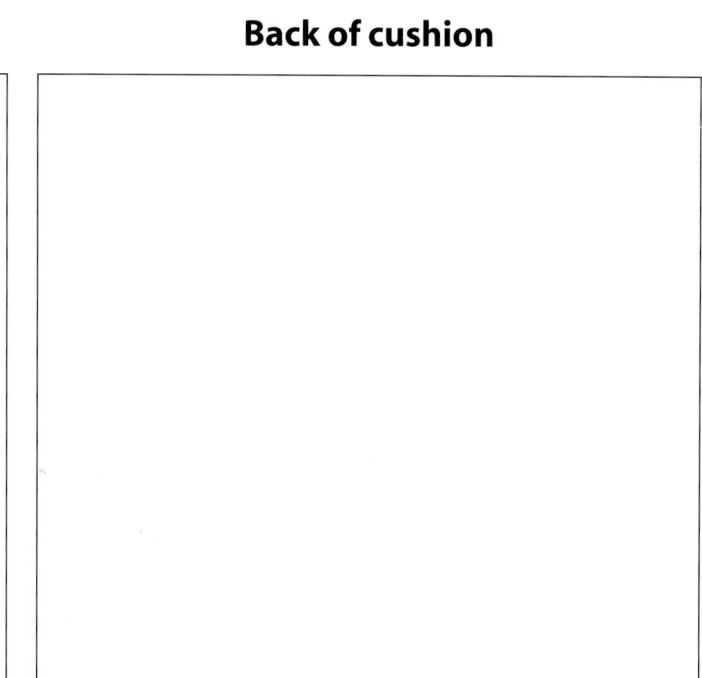

Back of cushion

56   Textiles 2   © Folens (copiable page)

Activity sheet – Accessories

Eco-friendly bags

👉 1 How eco-friendly are these bags? Cut out the cards and rank the bags according to the following criteria:

- Appearance (look, appeal)
- Usefulness to society
- How eco-friendly the bag is.

| Made from an animal feed bag |  Made from juice containers |  Made from organic cotton |
| 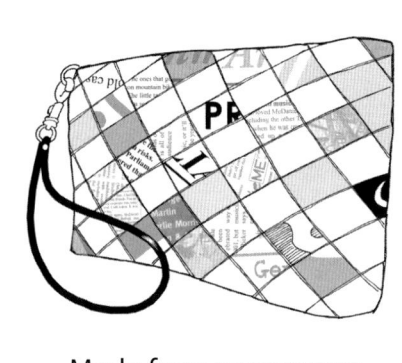 Made from newspaper |  Made from nylon fabric | Made from a coffee bean bag |

👉 2 After sorting the cards discuss the following questions with a partner.

Which bag is the most eco-friendly? Why? _____

_____

_____

Which bag would you choose for yourself? Why? _____

_____

_____

© Folens (copiable page)　　　　　Textiles 2

Teacher's notes

Labels and logos

Objectives

- To understand the purpose of labelling products
- To understand the information given on labels
- To know that some fabrics are made up of a blend of fibres and some of the reasons why
- To know that some companies use brand labels and logos
- To understand the importance of a product's country of manufacture
- To understand that design ideas can be protected by the inventor

Prior knowledge

Students should have completed some work on the properties of fabrics, basic marketing and environmental issues. It would be useful if they have some experience of using ICT, such as WordArt.

NC links

Key concepts: 1.4 Critical evaluation
Key processes: c, d
Range and content: a, c, e
Curriculum opportunities: a

Northern Ireland PoS

Skills: Use recognized symbols and drawing conventions

Scottish attainment targets

Needs and how they are met: Level E, Level F
Processes and how they are applied: Level C, Level D

Welsh PoS

Skills: Designing: 4, 8

Starter activity

Students could look at a range of labels from their own clothes or from some samples provided. They could compare the range of information presented and complete tally charts of information, such as country of manufacture or fabrics used.

Resource sheets and Activity sheets

The Resource sheet, 'Why blend fabrics?', looks at fabric blends and could be adapted to allow students to research the properties of synthetic fabrics if there are sufficient Internet facilities.

The Resource sheet, 'Labels explained', gives an example of a clothes label and explains what the information and different symbols mean.

The Activity sheet, 'Branding: logos', asks students to consider how they recognize famous brands and to add logos to some example products.

The Activity sheet, 'Design a logo', requires students to design a logo that they could use if they were a designer. This task encourages them to think about their name and initials and how they could be turned into a logo.

The Activity sheet, 'Air miles', requires students to consider where fabrics and products have come from.

Plenary

Students could discuss the work that they have completed as a class. They may be able to suggest further information that could be included on a label. They could discuss whether the label information would or should influence their choice of product.

Background

This unit explores the information that can be found on the labels of textile products. It looks closely at the reasons for the use of blended fibre textiles, at the use of logos to promote a brand and at some issues surrounding the country of manufacture.

Resource sheet – Labels and logos

Why blend fabrics?

On many labels you will see that a fabric is made from more than one material. Often, natural fibres such as wool or cotton are blended with a manufactured fibre such as polyester or Lycra™. This is because each type of fibre has different qualities and blending fibres can improve the finished fabric.

You will find some of these materials listed on the labels in your clothes:

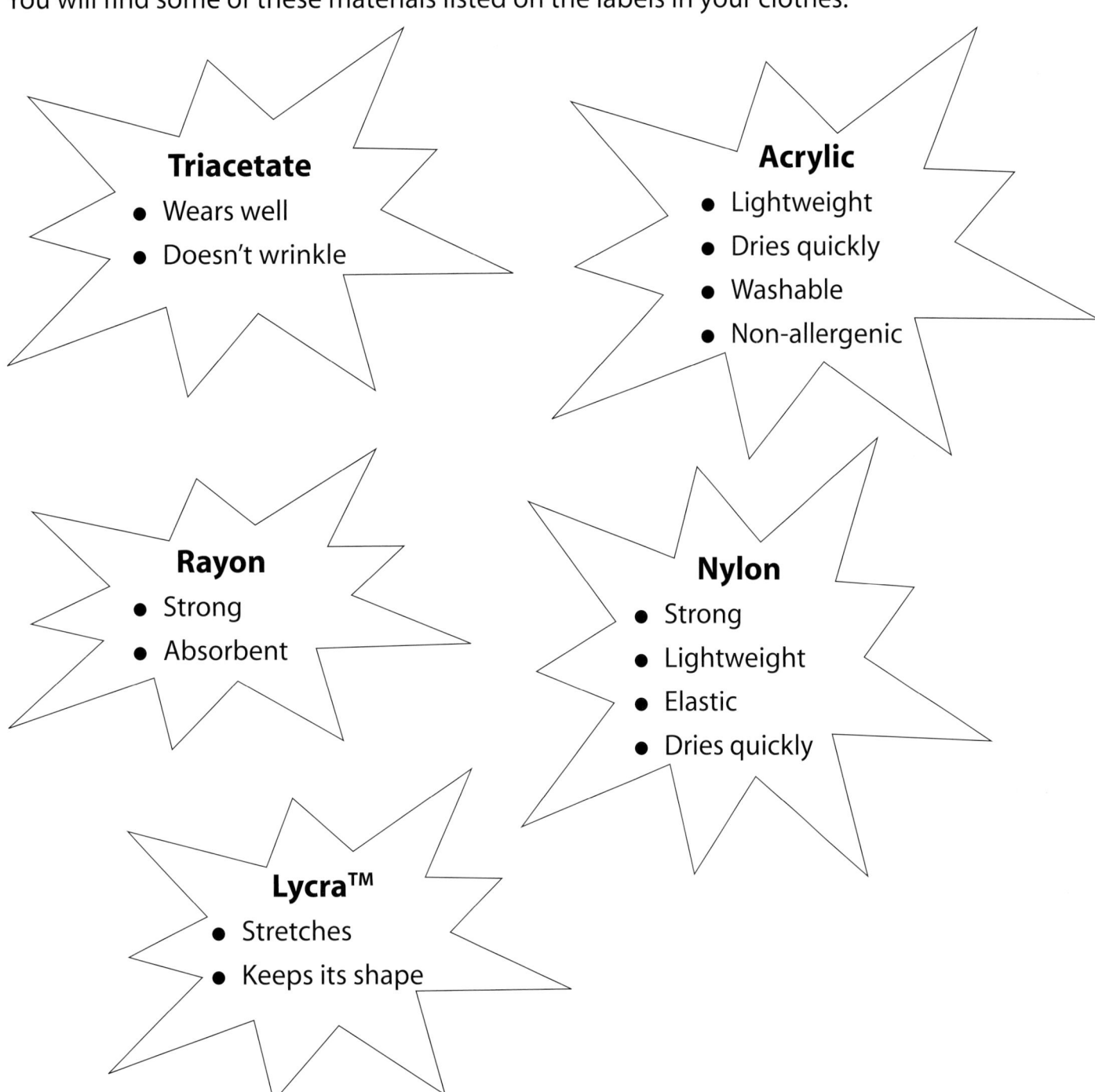

Triacetate
- Wears well
- Doesn't wrinkle

Acrylic
- Lightweight
- Dries quickly
- Washable
- Non-allergenic

Rayon
- Strong
- Absorbent

Nylon
- Strong
- Lightweight
- Elastic
- Dries quickly

Lycra™
- Stretches
- Keeps its shape

You could research other materials and their useful properties using the Internet.

Resource sheet – Labels and logos

Labels explained

Labels on textile products give a range of information that tells us about the product. They can help us care for the product and help us decide whether or not to buy it.

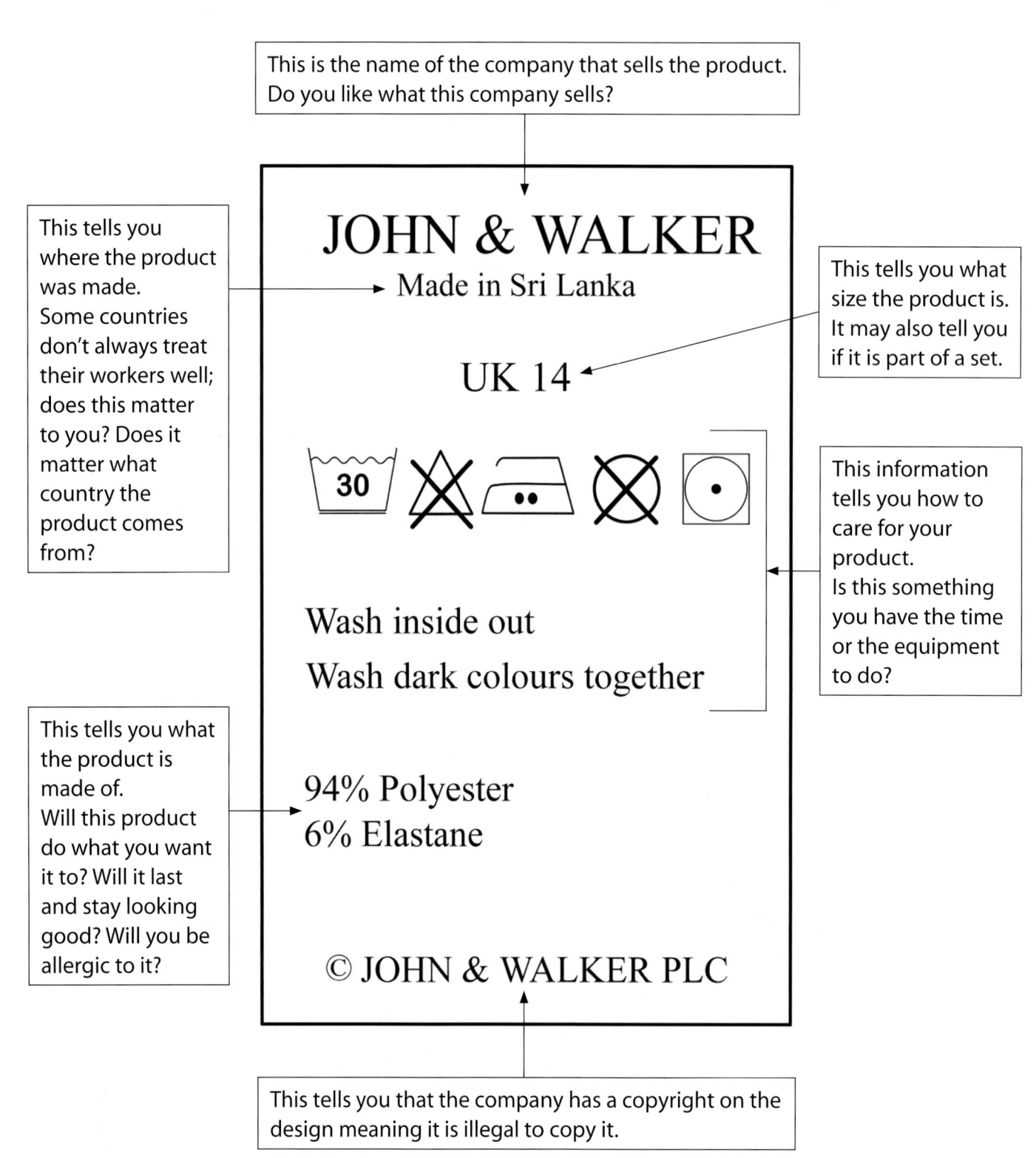

This is the name of the company that sells the product. Do you like what this company sells? → JOHN & WALKER

This tells you where the product was made. Some countries don't always treat their workers well; does this matter to you? Does it matter what country the product comes from? → Made in Sri Lanka

This tells you what size the product is. It may also tell you if it is part of a set. → UK 14

This information tells you how to care for your product. Is this something you have the time or the equipment to do? → [wash symbols: 30, do not bleach, iron medium, do not tumble dry, dry clean] / Wash inside out / Wash dark colours together

This tells you what the product is made of. Will this product do what you want it to? Will it last and stay looking good? Will you be allergic to it? → 94% Polyester / 6% Elastane

This tells you that the company has a copyright on the design meaning it is illegal to copy it. → © JOHN & WALKER PLC

The next time you buy a textile product, look at the label!

Activity sheet – Labels and logos

Branding: logos

☞ 1 Think of some famous fashion brands, such as Nike and Burberry. How do you recognize their products?

Many brands have a logo that appears on all their products. Some brands have their company name. Others choose a particular symbol or motif.

☞ 2 Choose a logo to add to each of the items below. You could choose your favourite designers or make up your own logos.

© Folens (copiable page)　　　Textiles 2

Activity sheet – Labels and logos

Design a logo

If you were a fashion designer, would you use your name on your products? What logo would be suitable? You may have a name that suggests a certain logo or theme such as Oaks, like the tree, or Taylor, like a tailor.

You could design a logo using your name, or your initials.

☞ Design your own logo in the space below.

Activity sheet – Labels and logos

Air miles

Textile labels tell us where a product was made and where the fabric came from. They often say 'Made in....'. If the product was made faraway, this could be bad for the environment as more fuel will be used to transport it.

1 Discuss with a partner whether you think it is better to buy products that have been made locally, or at least in the same country.

2 Look at the labels on a range of products. Use an atlas or the Internet to find the countries where the products were made. Try to find out how many air miles each product has travelled to reach the UK and plot them on the map. An example has been done for you.

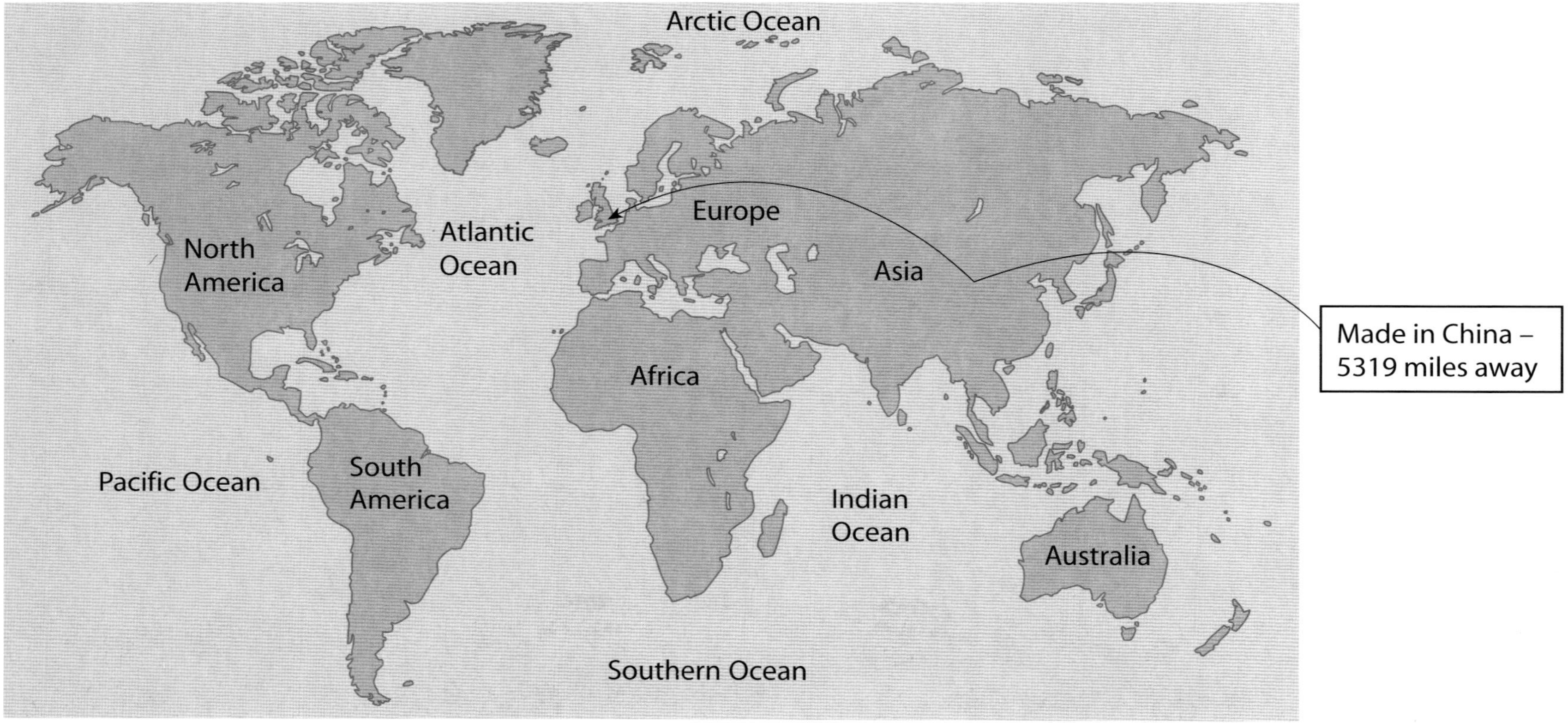

Made in China – 5319 miles away

Arctic Ocean
Europe
Asia
Africa
Indian Ocean
Australia
Southern Ocean
Atlantic Ocean
North America
South America
Pacific Ocean

3 Can you think of any other reasons why the country in which a product is made is important?

© Folens (copiable page)   Textiles 2   63

Assessment sheet – Textiles 2

☞ Tick a box next to each question to show how much help you needed with each task.

	I am…	With lots of help	With some help	With a bit of help	By myself
1	…able to find out information about my problem.				
2	…able to think of and draw several solutions to my problem.				
3	…able to decide which solution is the best one.				
4	…able to plan how to apply my solution to the problem.				
5	…able to make a prototype product of my solution.				
6	…able to test my prototype product.				
7	…able to show how I would make several products that look the same.				
8	…able to suggest improvements to my prototype product.				
9	…able to decide whether my prototype product solves my problem.				

To improve my design and technology skills I need to:

- _____

- _____

- _____